Commuters

COMMUTERS

A History of a British Way of Life

Simon Webb

PEN & SWORD
HISTORY

First published in Great Britain in 2016 by
Pen & Sword History
an imprint of
Pen & Sword Books Ltd
47 Church Street
Barnsley
South Yorkshire
S70 2AS

ISBN 978 1 47386 290 6

A CIP catalogue record for this book is
available from the British Library

Typeset in Ehrhardt by
Replika Press Pvt Ltd, India
Printed and bound in England
By CPI Group (UK) Ltd, Croydon, CR0 4YY

Pen & Sword Books Ltd incorporates the imprints of Pen & Sword
Archaeology, Atlas, Aviation, Battleground, Discovery, Family History,
History, Maritime, Military, Naval, Politics, Railways, Select, Social History,
Transport, True Crime, and Claymore Press, Frontline Books, Leo Cooper,
Praetorian Press, Remember When, Seaforth Publishing and Wharncliffe.

For a complete list of Pen & Sword titles please contact
PEN & SWORD BOOKS LIMITED
47 Church Street, (Barnsley: South Yorkshire, S70 2AS, England
E-mail: enquiries@pen-and-sword.co.uk
Website: www.pen-and-sword.co.uk

Contents

List of Plates

1. An invitation to Metro-land, a commuter's paradise.
2. The roots of the British commuting lifestyle lie buried 250 million years in the past.
3. The kind of slums from which early Victorian commuters wished to flee, by Gustave Doré.
4. The first fictional commuter, Bob Cratchit of Dicken's *A Christmas Carol*.
5. London Bridge to Greenwich, the world's first commuter railway.
6. One of the last brick kilns remaining in London, to be found in Holland Park.
7. *London going Out of Town – or The March of Bricks and Mortar*, by George Cruickshank.
8. Walter Hancock's *Automaton* in 1839, one of the first steam-driven buses in London.
9. Mr Pooter, hero of *The Diary of a Nobody*, putting up a plaster-of-paris stag's head.
10. The crowded interior of an early omnibus.
11. Working-class commuters arriving on an early-morning 'Parliamentary' workmen's train.
12. The last surviving fragment of London's once-extensive tramlines, in Southampton Row.
13. The Hansom cab, another popular means of transport for the wealthier commuter.
14. The dummy houses in London's Leinster Gardens that conceal the railway line.
15. Britain's first electric tram, at Northfleet in Kent in 1889.
16. The Aldersgate bombing of 1897.
17. A commuter's life in Golders Green, in a mock-Tudor semi.
18. The dream of many commuters: a typical mock-Tudor semi from the 1930s.
19. More examples of fine mock-Tudor properties for commuters.
20. Strap-hangers on the Tube in the rush hour.

Introduction

It is a way of life familiar to us all, if not from personal experience, then from television, books, films and newspapers. The rushed and frequently uncomfortable journey to work in the morning, undertaken on crowded trains or along gridlocked roads, followed by a similar ordeal when returning home at the end of the day. The daily grind of delays on the Tube, running to catch that vital train to the City or desperately seeking a parking space near the railway station or office. This then is all too often the typical lot and routine life of the British commuter. It is not today considered a particularly enviable or desirable lifestyle, certainly not one to which many people aspire. A large number of those caught up in it dream of the day that they can abandon what is sometimes called the 'rat race' for a calmer and less hectic existence. Little wonder that television comedies in the 1970s such as *The Good Life* and *The Fall and Rise of Reginald Perrin* enjoyed such popularity among commuters. This was Freudian wish fulfilment with a vengeance!

It is only relatively recently that people have regarded commuting as something from which they might wish to break free or escape. At one time, being a commuter was widely regarded as a worthy ambition. It was a respectable, stable and secure existence, with the prospect of owning a house in the suburbs and being able to tend a garden at the weekend. During the late nineteenth century, this comfortable way of life was, for many, the path to fulfilling their dreams. Even as late as the 1920s and 1930s, the suburban life of the commuter was held up as an admirable existence, one after which any right-thinking person might be expected to hanker. The Metropolitan Railway touted the dream of being a commuter between the wars, with a series of posters and booklets which have today more than a touch of bathos about them. One poster, advertising the supposed joys of what was known as Metro-land, depicted a bleak, monochrome streetscape. Below it was a rural scene of cottages and trees. Above the grim, serried ranks of city houses was the caption, 'Leave this', leading the eye down to the trees and grass. The slogan here was, 'Move to Edgware'. This poster may be seen in Illustration 1.

It is easy to laugh today at the notion that one might find fulfilment in moving to a London suburb such as Edgware, but at that time the idea of getting a house in the suburbs and being able to commute via the Underground to a job in the City really was an attractive one for many people. The poster described above, featured a few lines of prose by the seventeenth-century poet and essayist, Abraham Cowley: 'I never had any other desire so strong and so like to covetousness as that one which I have had always, that I might be Master of a small House and a Large garden, with moderate conveniences joined to them.' This, in a nutshell, summed up the dream that was being sold; that one might have a house and garden of one's own in a semi-rural location. That this idyll was being promoted by the Metropolitan Railway, meant by implication that part of the life being offered would entail regular journeys to work on the Underground. Edgware was essentially a commuters' paradise.

In the years following the end of the Second World War, the perception of living in the suburbs and commuting gradually changed. Instead of something to aim for, it became for many people something to be mocked and derided; a straitjacket, rather than a comfortable and reassuring life of routine and certainty. The commuter began to be seen as a little ridiculous; a stuffy and conventional figure, whose life was humdrum and dull. From the 1950s onwards, the archetypal commuter, with his pinstripe suit, bowler hat, tightly-furled umbrella and copy of *The Times* under his arm became a stock comic character on television and in cartoons. He represented the past, and not in a good way. In 1966, a satirical television programme, *The Frost Report*, showed a sketch which poked fun at the British class system. It featured Ronnie Corbett as a working-class man, wearing a cloth cap and muffler, Ronnie Barker as a middle-class individual in a trilby and John Cleese as an upper-class commuter, with the traditional bowler hat and umbrella. A few years later, *Monty Python's Flying Circus*, a ground-breaking comedy show, turned the bowler-hatted commuter into a comic stereotype. The programme also poked fun at suburban locations such as Surbiton and Purley. While this was going on on television, the magazine *Private Eye* was presenting the suburb of Neasden, in the heart of Metro-land, as another location full of commuters and deserving to be sneered at.

The typical view of commuters was that they were harried office workers, perpetually anxious about missing the train which will take them into town, men and women defined chiefly by their pattern of work. Not many people have seen the commuter as a significant figure in Britain's history; they are traditionally regarded more as extras. This is odd, because the contribution that commuting and commuters have made to British culture is immense, although it is has now been almost wholly forgotten. It is no exaggeration to say that in many ways, commuting has fashioned this country and, for good or ill, made it what it now is. One or two examples will make this clearer.

When Charles Darwin published *On the Origin of Species* in 1859, it caused an uproar, being widely denounced as blasphemous and irreligious. The book's general acceptance over the next few decades was greatly accelerated by the construction of railways and the building of suburbs for those who would be commuting by railway, both of which provided strong evidence for the veracity of Darwin's claims. It might even be said that the practice of commuting was indirectly instrumental in promoting the approval of Darwin's radical ideas. This ties in neatly with another instance of the way in which commuting has changed the intellectual life of the nation out of all recognition. In the early nineteenth century, books were an unaffordable luxury for all but the wealthiest men and women in Britain. Within a few decades, countless working-class men and women were not only buying books of their own or borrowing them from railway lending libraries, but had also acquired the leisure to read them for an hour or two each day. The consequences of this change in habits was momentous, leading to labourers educating themselves by reading Daniel Defoe, Charles Darwin and Karl Marx as they travelled to work each day. This too was a result of the increasing habit of commuting.

In this book, we shall be exploring the history of British commuters, seeing how and why this strange way of life developed and also the way in which the commuter became a risible figure; rather than a noble and heroic one. This concept will be examined in Chapter 3, as we look at fictional commuters and see how their portrayal in nineteenth-century fiction has shaped our view of commuters and commuting right up to the present day.

It is curious to note that there is no universally-accepted definition of what actually constitutes commuting or how we might identify a commuter and distinguish him from the man who walks to work a couple of streets from his home. Looking at the *Oxford English Dictionary* tells us, not very helpfully, that commuting is a matter of travelling 'some distance between one's home and place of work on a regular basis'. This is without a doubt true, but since all of us, other than those who work at home, are obliged to travel 'some distance' to work, it would seem to define commuters as being synonymous with employees. The Office for National Statistics is no more helpful, defining a 'regular commuter' as merely, 'a worker for whom a distance to work value has been calculated'. Using this definition leads the Office for National Statistics to classify over 80 per cent of the British population as commuters. A more useful means of classification is the one sometimes used when analysing data from the 2011 Census, which identifies workers who live in one local authority area and work in another. For the purposes of this book, we shall be elastic in our definition of what actually makes a commuter, according to circumstance.

Until a few years ago, most people had a clear idea of what constituted a commuter. Essentially, this would be a person who lived on the outskirts of a city or in the surrounding countryside and travelled into the centre of the city and back again every day to work. Not only this, but many of us also had a mental image of the typical commuter; a middle-aged man in a white-collar job, wearing a collar and tie. Although there are, by any definition, more commuters now in Britain than has ever been the case, there are grounds for supposing that the traditional commuter is a dying breed. That is to say that with anybody who travels any distance at all to a workplace being described officially as a 'regular commuter', the very concept of commuters is perhaps fading away. This idea will be explored in detail throughout this book.

Commuting, in the sense of travelling a considerable distance between home and place of work on a routine and regular basis, was unknown in Britain until the Industrial Revolution of the late eighteenth and early nineteenth centuries. The roots of commuting though lie buried a good deal further back in the past than the Georgian, Regency or Victorian eras. To find out how and why commuting began in this country, it will be necessary to travel back many millions of years, to a time 70 million years before the first dinosaurs stalked the Earth.

Before delving back millions of years in search of the origins of commuting, we might look at the derivation of the word itself; which is an importation from the United States. During the early days of the railways in America, companies running lines into cities such as New York, Boston and Chicago would offer a reduction, or 'commutation', of fares for those who travelled between two destinations more than once a day. The advantages for those living a few miles outside a city were immediately apparent and the scheme both appealed to existing residents living in the suburbs and also helped to encourage the creation of new suburbs, a phenomenon which also became frequent in Britain during the nineteenth and twentieth centuries. These 'commutation tickets' are what we know today as 'season tickets'. A process of back formation from the word 'commutation' gave rise to the expressions 'commuting' and 'commuters' being coined. In Britain, commuting has only been a commonly-used expression since the end of the Second World War.

Having established how the term 'commuting' arose, it is time to look into the origins of the practice itself, which are associated with a very early geological epoch; an age when insects and other invertebrates ruled the land and sky. Strange to relate, the pattern of commuting in Britain and the geographical locations in which the practice arose, were both directed by the conditions which existed on earth hundreds of millions of years ago.

Chapter 1

'Walking Suburbs': The Birth of Commuting

The evolution of the British custom of commuting to and from work each day is inextricably linked with events during the Carboniferous Era, over 300 million years ago. In the steamy swamps which covered the primeval continent of Gondwanaland at that time, both the temperature and the level of oxygen in the atmosphere were far higher than they are today. This allowed vast forests of towering club-moss, tree-ferns and horsetails to soar a hundred feet above the warm and waterlogged land below. The increased oxygen made it possible for insects too, to grow to enormous sizes. Millipedes two metres long scuttled around the detritus of the forest floor; competing for food with cockroaches the size of puppies. Overhead, dragonflies with wingspans which would rival that of a modern-day barn owl darted about. A forest of that era is shown in Illustration 2.

During the course of many millions of years, the giant mosses and ferns died and sank to the bottom of the shallow water which surrounded the soggy tracts of land. Layer upon layer accumulated in this way and in time, with the constant, restless shifting of the Earth's tectonic plates, were buried deep beneath the planet's surface. There, great heat and pressure wrought a miraculous transformation upon the decayed plant matter, turning it eventually into seams of brittle rock, consisting of between 80 and 90 per cent carbon. In the fullness of time, movements in the Earth's crust brought some of these reefs of shiny, black material to light again. We know this substance today as coal.

Nobody knows precisely when or where coal was first found to be a useful fuel. Certainly, the Romans were using it in the second and third centuries of the Common Era and by the medieval period it was being burnt for warmth by both the Chinese and also some tribes of Native Americans. It was not, however, until the beginning of the Industrial Revolution in Britain, during the eighteenth century, that large-scale exploitation of coal began. Before this time, it had been quarried from shallow pits; now, proper shafts were excavated deep into the ground and mining began in earnest. The furnaces and steam engines of the late eighteenth and early nineteenth centuries needed huge quantities of coal and it was only natural that industrialisation should have been closely associated with accessible deposits of this precious resource. Glancing at a geological survey of Britain shows that seams of coal found close enough to the surface to be readily available lie in the very areas where the Industrial Revolution was running at full speed; South Wales, Stoke, the Midlands, an arc stretching from Liverpool, through Manchester to Yorkshire, North East England and, in Scotland, around Glasgow and Edinburgh.

To understand what all this has to do with the first commuters, we need to look at the way of life in this country in the years preceding the Industrial Revolution. There have been settled communities in the British Isles since the beginning of the Neolithic Age some 6,000 years ago. These were either hamlets or villages; some of them approaching the size of small towns. There were no cities until the Roman conquest of Britain by Claudius in AD 43. Even after the building of the first cities, most people still lived in villages. Britain was to remain an agrarian society for another 2,000 years or so. Until as late as 1851, the majority of people in Britain lived in the countryside, there being few cities of any size until the nineteenth century. In 1790, only two English cities, London and Bristol, had populations greater than 50,000. Men and women worked on the land or made things in their own homes. Travel was undertaken rarely, because there was little public transport and the only way that the average person could get from one place to another was on foot. In such a society, people lived only a short walking distance from their place of work. The only reason most working people had to undertake longer journeys would be to move house or seek work. All this began to change irrevocably in the eighteenth century, when factories, foundries and blast furnaces began to spring up in certain areas of the country; principally those near to workable deposits of coal.

The manufacture of textiles was transformed within a few decades from a cottage industry into a large-scale operation powered by waterwheels and steam engines. The flying shuttle for looms, invented in 1733, the Spinning Jenny, devised thirty years later, along with various other developments in machinery such as steam engines, all tended towards the industrialisation of enterprises which had until that time been undertaken in people's homes or within small workshops. The increased demand for iron consequent upon all this, led to the proliferation of blast furnaces and the need for a continuous supply of coal, in the form of coke, to fuel them. It was this which in turn brought about the industrialisation and subsequent urbanisation of small towns such as Birmingham, Newcastle and Manchester. People flocked to these places because of the opportunities for work. The wages were better than those for farm labourers and, best of all, the work was not seasonal. Coal mining, iron smelting and the production of textiles in factories continued all year round.

In agriculture, there were slack periods when men and women were laid off and had no income for weeks, perhaps months, at a time. This was not the case with the new industries.

The industrial areas flourished and their populations increased exponentially. In the early eighteenth century, Manchester was a pretty market town with a population of around 10,000. By 1773, this had grown to 25,000 and then, within another fifteen years, had reached 42,000. By 1801, there were no fewer than 70,000 people living in Manchester and it had become one of the largest cities in England. The astonishing growth of cities such as Manchester, Birmingham and Liverpool was more in numbers of inhabitants rather than the area actually inhabited. Later on, throughout the nineteenth century, these cities would indeed expand spatially, engulfing the surrounding countryside, but to begin with people flocked to the new industrial towns and lived there as best they were able in the existing buildings. The results of this were disastrous from all points of view, beginning with the most appalling overcrowding. Property owners renting out rooms to recently-arrived workers from the country were, quite understandably, keen to maximise their profits. This was accomplished by cramming more and more tenants into existing accommodation. Often, this was done by 'making down' houses; subdividing them into ever small rooms. In lodging houses, it was not uncommon to find men sleeping five to a bed. Small rooms in slum districts might contain two families; each having four or five members. When every room was full to capacity, and it might reasonably have been thought that no more income could be extracted from a building; the landlords began offering cellars to rent. Like the Morlocks of H. G. Wells' *The Time Machine*, industrial workers were compelled to adopt a subterranean lifestyle. A census conducted in the port city of Liverpool in 1789 revealed that there were no fewer than 1,728 cellars in the town being used as living accommodation. Between them, these contained 6,788 people; some 12 per cent of the population of Liverpool. The situation was no better in Manchester. By the 1840s, the proportion of the working population in industrial cities who were living underground in cellars had increased, until in Liverpool, 20 per cent of working-class people were living in this way.

The terrible overcrowding was exacerbated by the almost complete lack of sanitary provisions. The poorer workers were dependent for water on a standpipe at a street corner, frequently only turned on for a short period each day. A single lavatory might be shared by anything up to sixty or even 100 people. Such conditions were a breeding-ground for diseases of all types. Epidemics of scarlet fever, tuberculosis, typhoid, dysentery and smallpox swept the cities of eighteenth and nineteenth century Britain with monotonous regularity. Some health problems, bronchitis and rickets for example, were endemic. It will come as no surprise to learn that the life expectancy of a working-class person in the centre of Manchester or Birmingham was half that of the typical agricultural worker. We saw earlier that a geological map of Britain showed a direct correlation between deposits of coal and the areas of greatest industrialisation. An epidemiological map, one indicating infant mortality rates, would have shown a precisely similar pattern, with the highest death rates clustered around South Wales, Newcastle, Birmingham, Manchester, Glasgow and Edinburgh. Large cities were not healthy places to be living at that time, especially for babies and children.

The appalling stench from the crowded streets, courts and alleyways in the middle of cities at this time was believed to be a mortal hazard in itself to those living near enough to smell it. There were, in the mid-nineteenth century, two chief theories about the transmission of disease. Apart from the idea of contagion by germs, there was a strong school of thought which held that illness was caused by 'miasma'. In effect, it was the bad air which rose from decomposing or filthy organic matter which spread disease and if you could smell something rotten or foul, then you were likely to develop an illness as a result. Even Florence Nightingale was a believer in this notion and it meant that many middle class people were frightened of living in close proximity to squalor, lest they developed cholera in consequence of catching a whiff of the slums borne to them on a breeze!

Although there was no clear idea of the true nature of disease during those early years of the Industrial Revolution, it was obvious to those with money that living cheek-by-jowl with the poverty-stricken in the heart of a city like Manchester, or even London, was not a healthy option. Already, by the end of the eighteenth century, wealthy Londoners were moving to the western edge of the city, near Hyde Park, the district which was to become known as the West End. Quite apart from considerations of health, there was the purely aesthetic matter of not wishing to live in a smoky part of London which stank abominably. With only open sewers and rivers available for the disposal of human excrement and all other filth, the smell in the crowded parts of big cities at that time was all but unendurable. The use of coal was increasing year by year, which meant that even new buildings were soon blackened and begrimed with soot and sulphurous deposits.

Accounts of living conditions in the hearts of British cities in the first half of the nineteenth century are unbelievably grim. Friedrich Engels, in his *The Condition of the Working Class in England in 1844*, described how factory workers in Manchester were existing at that time. He visited some slums, in what we would today call the 'Inner City' and wrote: 'On reaching them one meets with a degree of dirt and revolting filth the like of which is not to be found elsewhere ... In one of these courts, just at the entrance where the covered passage ends, there is a privy without a door. This privy is so dirty that the inhabitants of the court can only enter or leave the court if they are prepared to wade through puddles of stale urine and excrement.' Engels went on to describe the conditions in the homes, many of which had only earth floors, and also the appalling state of the nearby river, which was bubbling with industrial effluent and human waste. The further from such filthy places that one could live, the better.

The desire to live a little outside cities for reasons of health, was not a new one. In 1689, William III moved into Kensington Palace, at that time in the open countryside: the smoky air of the capital had caused his asthma to become troublesome. It was not only respiratory disorders such as asthma and bronchitis which could be precipitated or made worse by the atmosphere of Britain's cities as the Industrial Revolution gathered pace. Even deficiency diseases such as rickets became prevalent among children brought up close to the centres of cities. Problems of this sort associated with living in cities persisted well into the twentieth century. In the 1950s, there were, on average, thirty-eight hours of sunshine in London during November. Today, the figure is seventy hours. This has nothing to do with climate change, but is a direct consequence of the Clean Air Act of 1956, which forbade the burning of coal in domestic grates. Bright sunlight was simply unable to penetrate the clouds of smoke and soot particles which were suspended above the capital. The lack of sunshine before this time meant that many children did not have enough Vitamin D, which is synthesised in the body only when ultra-violet light falls on the skin. The result was many cases of rickets, in which the bones remain soft and prone to deformation. This disorder was horribly common in industrial areas where the smoke from both factories and houses obscured the light of the sun.

It was all very well for the royal, aristocratic or wealthy to set up home a few miles from the insalubrious centres of cities, but what of those who were compelled to work there? For the ordinary labourers and factory workers of course, there was no choice in the matter. Just as in the countryside, they had to live as close as possible to their place of work. For other workers though, managers, bookkeepers and the emerging class of commercial clerks, things were a little more promising. Cities such as Manchester, Birmingham and even London might have rapidly-growing populations, but they were not yet expanding physically. Only three or four miles from the centre of Manchester were little villages, which would be far more pleasant places to live than the dirty, smoky and cramped centre; with all its attendant disadvantages. A healthy man can walk those three or four miles each morning and evening in no more than an hour or hour and a quarter. This extra time spent in travelling was a small price to pay for the vast improvement in lifestyle that a home in a suburb or village outside the city boundaries would bring.

We must of course bear in mind that there was almost no public transport of any kind, other than stagecoaches travelling between cities, at that time. There were short-stage coaches running between villages on the outskirts of London, such as Camberwell or Paddington, into the centre of town, but these were too expensive for most people to consider using twice a day to get them to and from work. Typically, the fares were 6d (2½p) a journey and using such a means of transport to commute every day would have taken more than half the average clerk's wages. There were also Hackney carriages, but these were even more expensive to hire. Running one's own carriage and horses would require a stable and grooms, far beyond the means of anybody other than perhaps a factory owner or member of the gentry. For the ordinary person, the only means of transport to work was likely to be walking. These first commuters were therefore pedestrians.

It is important to bear in mind that the use of the expression 'commuting' in connection with British workers two centuries ago is a little anachronistic. Nobody in this country would have thought of himself as a 'commuter' until the 1930s or 1940s at the earliest. Nevertheless, for want of a convenient synonym, we shall use the words 'commuter' and 'commuting', asking only that readers are aware that nobody in nineteenth-century Britain would have thought of himself in such terms.

Most of us have fixed in our minds the image of commuters as travelling into cities either by public transport or car. The idea of walking to work from the suburbs would be seen as perverse today, but this is only because the cities in this country now sprawl over such great areas as to make this mode of travel impractical. It is worth remembering that as late as 1939, the year that the Second World War began, more people commuted by foot into central London than used trains or buses. Today, this would hardly be sensible. Walking to an office in central London from an outer suburb such as Goodmayes, on the fringes of Essex, would entail a journey of ten miles or so. Few of us would wish to spend six or seven hours a day walking briskly, in addition to eight hours in an office! Until the early years of Victoria's reign though, commuting on foot was very much the rule.

In the later eighteenth and early nineteenth century, rows of houses, often terraces of townhouses, were built around the edges of many British cities. These properties were intended not so much for the very wealthy, but more for the new 'middling sort', people we would today describe as middle class. This housing meant that those with a little more money could live far enough from the slums which lay at the hearts of the cities, that they would not be forced to encounter the ghastly scenes about which Engels had written. Typical inner-city slums are shown in Illustration 3. These districts of decent properties were on the outskirts of cities and they became known, for obvious reasons, as 'walking suburbs'. This was the very beginning of commuting in Britain, the clerks and other white-collar workers in these new streets walking to their offices in the city centres and then making their way home on foot at the end of the day.

In addition to the novels which he wrote, Charles Dickens was a keen observer of London life, and his vivid sketches of life on the streets of the capital tell us a lot about British society during the Victorian Era. In *Sketches by Boz*, first published in book form in 1836, Dickens writes of the morning rush hour of commuters in London, in the days before there was any public transport to speak of. He described the, 'early clerk population of Somers and Camden Towns, Islington and Pentonville', as they were, 'fast pouring into the City'. These, according to Dickens, were 'middle-aged men, whose salaries have by no means increased in the same proportion as their families' and he tells us how he watched them 'plod steadily along, apparently with no object in view but the counting-house'. Except that these commuters were on foot, rather than travelling by Tube, this scene has a timeless air about it.

An articled clerk at a firm of attorneys in the City of London in 1820 wrote in his diary that both his employers walked to the office each day. One lived in Islington and the other across the river in Walworth. Both used to walk to work, arriving at the office not a minute later than half past nine. Not all the walking suburbs of this kind were in London, nor were all those who lived in them clerical workers. One of the things which tends sometimes to be forgotten is that a very large proportion of Victorian commuters, especially once efficient public transport had been established, were manual workers. Even before that time, in some cities the walking suburbs were more a working-class phenomenon than was often the case in London. The Welsh port city of Cardiff, for instance, had districts such as Grangetown and Newtown. Dockers and labourers, many of them Irish, lived in those parts of the city and walked to work at the docks each morning. In London though, these early commuters were more often than not working in offices and for an understanding of the lifestyle of such men, we cannot do better than turn once again to Charles Dickens, who provided us with a memorable fictional example of such a commuter from a walking suburb.

One of the best-loved of all Charles Dickens' books is *A Christmas Carol*, first published in 1843, just five years after Queen Victoria ascended the throne. We are all of us familiar with the miserly Ebenezer Scrooge and his put-upon clerk, Bob Cratchit, who, together with his family, may be seen in Illustration 4. Bob Cratchit, father to that most famous of cripples to be found in literature, Tiny Tim, carried out routine clerical work at Scrooge's office in the City of London. We are told that he was copying letters there on Christmas Eve. Scrooge's business was perhaps in one of the little alleyways and courts near the Bank of England and Royal Exchange. After leaving work, Bob Cratchit joined a group of boys on a slide going down Cornhill, which fixes the location of his place of work fairly accurately. When he had finished larking around with the boys in the vicinity of Cornhill, he then, 'ran home to Camden Town as hard as he could pelt, to play at blind man's buff'.

Bob Cratchit is the first commuter to be described in fiction and examining him and his life in a little detail will give us some insight into the life led by a typical commuter at this time Dickens was famously accurate in his writing of London and its denizens, some of his earliest work consisting, as we have seen, of real-life sketches of London life. His portrait of an early example of a commuting commercial clerk is likely to be a faithful one. At the time that he was writing *A Christmas Carol,* the London district of Camden was on the very edge of London, fringed with fields and open country. It would be the ideal spot for a white-collar worker who wished to place a little distance between his family and the unhealthy slums of central London. This was a time when it was by no means uncommon for an entire family to live in one room of a house. Sometimes, they would be forced to share their room with another family. By contrast, we are told that in the case of Bob Cratchit, 'the Ghost of Christmas Present blessed his four-roomed house'! Granted that the Cratchits had six children, but even so, an entire house to themselves would have been considered a rare luxury to many of the poorer citizens of London at that time.

Both Bob Cratchit and his master, Scrooge, were examples of an emerging phenomenon in British society. Neither were aristocrats, nor were they common labourers. They belonged to what had, since early in the eighteenth century been referred to as the 'middling sort'. This term, which was eventually replaced by 'middle class', was applied to everybody below the aristocracy and above manual workers. It included doctors, priests, lawyers, teachers, shopkeepers, bankers and governesses, among others. Members of this class ranged from rich landowners who had made their money in trade, all the way down to humble and low-paid curates. Some of the 'middling sort' might have more money than most aristocrats, others could be earning less than a skilled artisan. An increasing number, as the nineteenth century drew on, were clerks and office workers.

Bob Cratchit was frankly poor; we are told several times in the text that he earned only fifteen shillings (75p) a week. This would be less than a carpenter or other skilled manual worker might typically be bringing home each week. One thing that the Cratchits would have though, which could not always be measured in purely financial terms, was status. The fact that the family lived in a suburb automatically raised them above the slum dwellers of the East End. That the head of the household worked in an office, rather than unloading ships in the docks or swinging a pickaxe, also meant that Bob Cratchit and his family had a tenuous, but nevertheless real, claim to belong to the 'middling sort'.

The movement of white-collar workers and others who did not work with their hands to the outer fringes of the cities was similar in many ways to the modern phenomenon which has sometimes been called 'white flight'. This entailed predominantly white, middle-class families moving away from the inner residential areas of British cities in order to escape the supposed deterioration in quality of life caused by immigration. The poor conditions in the inner districts of cities was the main the factor which motivated those of the 'middling sort' to head out for the suburbs during and after the Industrial Revolution. Health was one concern, but there were others, two of which have a very modern flavour. The first was the high levels of crime found in and about the poorer parts of industrial cities. Muggings and burglaries are not new crimes and were common enough in Georgian and Victorian times. They were both crimes more commonly committed by the poor against those better off than themselves. A second fear of middle-class people living near to the slums was an anxiety about what might perhaps be called moral contagion.

Because of the terrible crowding in the hearts of cities at that time, including London, there was a suspicion among 'respectable' people that all this sharing of rooms and even beds by unrelated men, women and children led to unbridled promiscuity. There may perhaps have been something in this; at the very least, such living conditions would not have been conducive to Victorian notions of propriety and modesty. Children would routinely witness their parents having sex and there was far less prudishness about sex and bodily functions among slum dwellers than there was in families who lived in larger houses with more privacy. It was thought that the sort of life led by people in such cramped conditions could create an unhealthy and immoral atmosphere and that bringing up a family in close proximity to those living such lives would be hazardous to the religious and moral state of children's minds. So it was that there was a desire to keep a distance from such goings on, by removing themselves physically from the locality.

Before the coronation of Queen Victoria, the situation may be summed up in this way. The populations of the large towns were growing rapidly, in some cases doubling in twenty years. This caused those who could afford it, or who had sufficient get-up-and-go, to move out to either the suburbs or even the countryside beyond the boundary of the city or town itself. This happened in Manchester and Birmingham, where some of the residents moved first to the edge of the city and then to villages a few miles further out. Unfortunately for them though, another process was now at work. Having watched the existing property become absolutely full of tenants, it was plain to most people that there was literally no more room for people to live. It was physically impossible to cram any more people into the houses which were already standing and yet more and more people were still drifting into the cities in search of work. This caused a great and continuing burst of development, which precipitated something of a crisis for those of the new middle class who had established themselves outside the working-class districts.

There was an inexhaustible demand for new workers as more and more factories, mills, foundries, mines and docks were established. Since there really was no more space in the housing stock which was already being used, there was nothing for it but to build new homes for these workers. Not unnaturally, those responsible for the construction of the new houses wished to erect them as quickly and cheaply as possible, squeezing as many properties into as small an area as could be achieved. In a typical area of such slum housing, there would be seventy houses to an acre. These days, twelve is more usual. In the great majority of such developments, there was no provision for sewers and only limited access to running water. Those building these cheap properties hoped that the local authorities would eventually lay drains and sewers, but even if they did not, by that time there would be new projects under way and little chance of any complaints from the poverty-stricken factory workers and miners would be occupying the property.

Many of these new houses were of the 'back-to-back' type, which can still be seen today in the former industrial and mining areas of South Wales and Northern England. These developments were slums from the very beginning. Such streets of terraced houses spread rapidly out from the cities, encroaching first on the existing suburbs and then into the countryside. Those who had moved into picturesque little villages far from the noise and smoke of the city, found themselves surrounded by slum housing. This in turn caused an exodus of middle-class and white-collar workers even further out.

This expansion of the new, enlarged towns and cities caused created a problem for commuters. Until now, it had been possible to walk to and from work, the journey not taking more than an hour and a half at most. Once you start allocating more than this for your journey to work in the morning though, you will find yourself spending too much of the working day in travel. Not only that, but after a walk of more than five miles or so to work in the morning and the same exertion again in the evening, after a day's work, and you might well start wondering about the length of time you have left at the end of the day. When compiling the census, the American government includes a category for what they are pleased to call 'extreme commuting'. This is defined as any journey to or from work exceeding an hour and a half.

It is perhaps one thing to spend an hour and a half or two hours travelling to work if you have a high-powered job which enables you to live a comfortable, perhaps even luxurious, lifestyle in the evenings and at weekends. Bankers and businessmen routinely commute into London from a hundred or more miles away, rising at five or six in the morning to do so. It is quite another matter if your job is a routine and humdrum one. Then, the law of diminishing returns comes into play and some who are making such a long journey twice a day will begin to ask themselves if it is all worthwhile and whether they wouldn't be better off finding a job closer to their home. The stage was set for the modern commuter to make his appearance – the person who catches the train, tube or bus in the morning and makes his way into the city by public transport. We will, in the next chapter, be looking at how the world of modern commuting began; the rise of the commuter who travels to work and back by various types of wheeled vehicles.

First though, we must reflect upon the surprising fact that for all the changes in urban environment at which we have been looking, walking to work is today still more popular than the use of buses or coaches for commuting. It is in fact the second only to driving as the most popular means of getting to work. The 2011 census showed that 2.8 million people in England and Wales walk to work every day, as opposed to the 1.9 million who travel by bus or coach. London Tube trains and other light rail transport methods such as the trams of Sheffield and Newcastle's Metro, are only used by a million commuters regularly; the walking commuter is not yet quite extinct, nor likely to be for a little while yet.

Chapter 2

Paddle Steamers and Steam Trains: The Start of Public Transport in Cities

In the previous chapter, we looked at the way in which the climatic and geological conditions in the remote past exercised a direct and profound influence on patterns of work in Britain 300 million years later. This is not the only example of the way in which a relatively minor shifting of the tectonic plates which form the Earth's crust have had a bearing upon the development of commuting in this country.

Over 250 million years after the end of the Carboniferous Era, although still a very long time ago, large parts of the British Isles lay at the floor of an ancient sea. Rivers drained into this sea via estuaries and deltas, flooding it with silt and minute particles of rock which had been eroded from the rocks which lined their banks. These tiny fragments of rock were too small to be seen with the naked eye, each one being no larger than a five-hundredth of a millimetre in size. The billions upon billions of microscopic grains gradually settled on the bottom of the ocean, where, over countless thousands of years, they formed a layer of slippery mud. Millions of years later, these immense deposits of mud were raised from the seabed and became part of the dry land. Water drained from them and they solidified into the stiff, moist substance that we call clay. Technically, this is a type of sedimentary rock called argillaceous rock. It belongs to the same general category as shale and sandstone. If dug from the ground and left to dry naturally, clay becomes brittle, crumbly and friable. However, if it is heated to a great temperature, it becomes a hard, durable and weatherproof material which is eminently suitable for building.

By the time that Victoria became Queen in 1838, the slums at the centre of the great cities and new industrial areas of Britain were full to capacity. The working families began to move outwards, colonising the fringes of cities; districts which had previously been fairly well ordered and 'respectable'. The more affluent, who lived nearby, began to decamp further out, but this created a problem. The villages a few miles from cities soon became popular with those fleeing the crowded and pestilential slums which seemed to be expanding like rapidly-spreading stains, but there were only a limited number of houses in such places. Britain was in the grip of a population explosion, which took place almost entirely in urban areas, and however densely one packed the existing houses with new tenants, there was eventually no more room. The only option was for the cities to expand physically into the countryside.

The growth of a village or town was, before the time at which we are looking, a steady, slow and organic business. The population increased as children were born or strangers moved into a district. This would be offset by the deaths of older inhabitants and people leaving to live elsewhere. Any slight increase in the number of people living in a town could be accommodated by the building of the occasional new house. Some were constructed of wattle and daub, others, in areas like the Chilterns and Cotswolds, of stone. It was little matter that hewing blocks of stone from a quarry and shaping them, or felling trees, seasoning the timber and then producing a half-timbered house from it were both painstakingly slow processes; there was no particular hurry. Now though, in the wake of the Industrial Revolution, there *was* a hurry. With the unprecedentedly rapid growth of cities such as London, Birmingham and Manchester, there was a desperate need for new houses. Just as textiles and other goods were now being mass produced, rather than being carefully crafted by patient and skilled artisans, so too would it be necessary to create rapidly and efficiently, many tens of thousands of new houses over a short space of time. The production of housing to accommodate those participating in the Industrial Revolution, would itself need to be industrialised. The obvious, indeed only, medium suitable for such needs was brick.

Producing bricks is really very simple. A few feet below the topsoil in many parts of the country lie deposits of brickearth and clay. These are the remnants of ancient seafloors and lakebeds. All one needs to do is shape this material into rectangular blocks and then fire these in kilns. Sometimes, other substances can be mixed with the clay to give it different colours, textures or qualities; but that is really all that there is to making bricks. The raw material is free and just need to be taken from the ground. Some of the things which were mixed with the brickearth not only helped with the process of firing, but also disposed of refuse. Domestic cinders and ashes, which were mainly coal ash, for instance, meant that the bricks became in effect self-firing. There was enough flammable material left in cinders to ensure that one could generate sufficient heat to fire bricks without the use of kilns. In short, the brick makers of the Industrial Revolution both produced vital building material, while at the same time getting rid of the vast quantities of coal ash which were generated by the domestic and industrial use of coal.

Fortunately, London lies on a vast sea of clay, and so do many other parts of the country, so anywhere where houses were needed in and around most of the capital: all that was required was to dig a large hole and take out as much of the substance as was needed. The same applied to other parts of Britain where the Industrial Revolution was in full swing. This is why, since those early days of suburban building, commuters have lived in brick houses.

The use of brick for housebuilding grew side by side with the exploitation of the medium for industrial purposes, the construction of factories, mills, railway stations and viaducts, for example. As this process accelerated, it became increasingly apparent that as the cities of Britain began to sprawl outwards, that those wishing to work in the centre would need another method of travel, other than simply using their feet. Once suburbs were being thrown up more than three or four miles from the centre of a city, it was no longer practical for men and women to walk into town to work. These new residential districts were not walking suburbs, but places which required a new way of thinking about urban transport: a reliance upon some mode of travel other than foot.

It might have been thought that the railway companies which were springing up all over Britain at that time would have been quick to exploit the newly-created need for affordable transport in and around cities. In general, they were not. The prevailing view of railways was that they were very useful for carrying freight and a limited number of passengers from one city to another in a hurry, but that once there, the old methods of horses and carriages, short-stage coaches and of course pedestrianism were sufficient to meet most needs. The idea that one might regularly travel only a few miles by railways, from the outer fringes of a city to its centre and back again in a day, was a strange one and took some little time for the companies fully to grasp. When the London to Birmingham railway line began to run, for instance, the first stop from central London was not until Harrow, which was eleven miles away. The railways were intended to connect one city with another, not one district of a city with a relatively nearby area. In short, commuter traffic was thought to have a negligible potential for the new means of transport. This was strange, because the very first steam railway for passengers in London had been built specifically to cater for commuters.

The first public railway to run in Britain, from Stockton to Darlington, began services in September 1825. It was a great success and initiated a boom, with rival companies springing up almost every day, all with schemes of their own. One of these was the London and Greenwich Railway Company, which was launched on 25 November 1831. This was designed to carry passengers from the suburbs of Greenwich and Deptford, south of the Thames, in Kent, into the heart of the capital. The terminus was to be at London Bridge, thus providing handy access to the City of London, by simply crossing London Bridge on foot. An Act of Parliament was necessary before the railway could be built and this was passed in 1833, following which construction of the line began.

The railway from Greenwich to London was not only the first passenger railway in London and the first commuter line anywhere; it was also to be the first elevated railway line ever built anywhere in the world. Because of the technical difficulties which building a series of level crossings through built-up areas such as Bermondsey would have entailed, it was decided to run the entire three-and-a-half mile line on one long viaduct. The result was a masterpiece of Victorian engineering; over 800 arches, which is still the longest construction of its type in Britain. This may be seen in Illustration 5.

It is curious sometimes to speculate on how the world might have been, had things turned out just a little differently. We view railway viaducts and their arches today as ugly, strictly functional necessities, structures in whose shadow nobody in his senses would choose to live. We know that garages and light industry might utilise the arches of a railway viaduct, but imagine building your house inside one of them! Illustration 3 is an etching by Gustave Doré which shows how railway viaducts complemented and increased the squalor of the slums of nineteenth-century Britain. When the Greenwich Viaduct was constructed though, the original idea was to build houses in all the arches and then use the viaduct as the basis for a boulevard of shops and inexpensive housing. Only a few houses were actually built and those living in them claimed that the noise of the trains running over their heads was no more disagreeable than the rumble of distant thunder.

The notion of railway viaducts becoming attractive and desirable features of the urban environment did not really catch on and they were destined to be regarded as eyesores, wherever they sprang up. What certainly did catch on, though, was the idea of a short railway line which linked the centre of the city with districts three or four miles away. On the Whit Monday Bank Holiday of the year that the London and Greenwich Railway began running public services in 1836, an almost unbelievable 13,000 passengers were carried on one day alone. Within eight years, a million and a half passengers were travelling on the line each year, at an average fare of 6d (2½p). Spending a shilling a day on transport to and from work was more than many people could afford to pay, but wealthy businessmen in Greenwich and Blackheath found the line a boon in carrying them to the edge of the City of London in a matter of minutes.

Thinking presumably of those living in the so-called walking suburbs, the company operating the Greenwich and London line constructed a pedestrian path running along the viaduct, next to the railway line. For a 1d (½p) toll, people could walk to London Bridge Station along this raised walkway. So popular was the railway though, that it soon proved more profitable to close down the pedestrian 'boulevard', as it was called at the time, and replace it with another railway line. Despite the enormous number of people using the line to Greenwich, including many commuters, the companies promoting new lines took some time to be persuaded of the economic advantages to them of catering for short-distance journeys made by train. This initially left the fast-growing commuter trade to be exploited by buses and coaches running along the ordinary roads. One effect that the building of the three-and-a-half mile viaduct did have was to create a shortage of bricks for other building work in the capital. The 400 navvies working on the project were using over 100,000 bricks a day, the whole job eventually taking 60 million bricks to complete. Building in London slowed down noticeably for a few months while work was taking place.

The development of commuter suburbs was continuing at a frantic pace across the whole of Britain; with new rows of houses springing up on the edge of big cities and towns. This development was patchy and unplanned; the twin driving forces being the greed of speculators and the needs of the new, urban workforce. Sometimes, new slums would engulf a previously green and leafy area. This happened outside Manchester. Better-off citizens who had moved out of the centre of the city to escape the factories and shocking living conditions of the sort about which Friedrich Engels wrote, found that their comfortable villas were engulfed almost overnight by new streets of mean little back-to-back workers' terraces; forcing them to flee even further outward, into the countryside. On other occasions, the opposite happened and those living in slums would find themselves being surrounded by smart new homes intended for the well-to-do. The north London district of Notting Hill provided a good example of this latter phenomenon.

In the early part of the nineteenth century, a notorious slum lay to the north of Holland Park. It occupied what is today one of the most fashionable and expensive parts of London; an upmarket part of Notting Hill which was at that time known as the 'Potteries and Piggeries'. The piggeries part of the name came from the fact that as parts of the West End became smarter and more respectable, the practice of pig-keeping was discouraged and so those who had kept pigs around Marble Arch decamped west, settling near Notting Hill. The relentless march of the new suburbs pursued them though and it was not long before brick makers moved into the area as well; which is where the 'Potteries' part of the district's name comes from. Pits were dug, clay excavated and the newly-formed bricks baked in beehive kilns which dotted the landscape. One survives to this day in Holland Park and may be seen in Illustration 6. As the bricks were produced, they were used to build new houses and little by little, as the stylish new villas were completed and then occupied by the wealthier type of commuter, the slum dwellers were forced to move even further out.

This ceaseless advance of housing, most of which was to be for commuters, was satirised by George Cruikshank in a cartoon published in 1829 entitled *London going Out of Town – or The March of Bricks and Mortar*. Cruikshank, who went on to illustrate many of Charles Dickens' books, showed an army on the march; an army which was desolating and destroying the countryside. This may be seen in Illustration 7. Hods full of cement move forward like infantry, while brick kilns of the sort which we saw in Illustration 6 serve as artillery, firing showers of bricks into open fields, while haystacks flee in terror. Half-built houses consolidate this victory.

The constant demand for bricks, combined with the new railway lines which were quartering the country, had a curious by-product, which was the confirmation of Charles Darwin's shocking new theory of evolution. These days, we view anybody who believes that the Earth was literally created and populated with animals and plants in the brief period of six days some 6,000 years ago as being a dyed-in-the-wool fundamentalist. We have even coined a derogatory term for such fanatics; we call them creationists.

Until the Industrial Revolution, the world was seen as a fairly stable and changeless place. There hadn't really been *time* for it to change. Using the genealogies found in the Bible, the seventeenth-century Primate of All Ireland, Bishop James Ussher, had calculated that the earth had been formed on 23 October 4004 BC. Dr John Lightfoot, Vice-Chancellor of the University of Cambridge and a contemporary of Bishop Ussher's, managed to narrow the moment of creation down even further and established by close examination of Scripture that, 'man was created by the Trinity on October 23 4004 B.C. at nine o'clock in the morning'. The Earth had continued in more or less the same form for the next 6,000 years; with all animals and plants remaining just as they had been created. When Charles Darwin's *On the Origin of Species* was published in 1859, the ideas which it contained were very disturbing to many devout churchgoers. Obviously, if the book was true, then the evolution of all the different species to be seen in nature must have taken vastly longer than a mere 6,000 years. The implication was that God had not created animals like lions and tigers, horses and oxen, birds and fishes as we now know them, but that they had evolved from earlier and more primitive animals. This is of course in direct contravention of Scripture, which specifically claims that God created cattle and whales in the same week that He made the first man and woman. Darwin's ideas caused great controversy.

Fortunately, quite a few naturalists were already prepared for the revelation that the earth was actually far older than suggested by Bishop Ussher's chronology. By using the evidence of their eyes during visits to brick fields, such men were aware that it was inconceivable that the world had only been in existence for a few thousand years. Indirectly, the increase in commuting and suburban living had provided the evidence that enabled everybody to see for themselves just why Darwin was probably right and the Bible wrong when it came to the age of the Earth.

From the 1820s onwards, brick fields or, as they were also known, brick-pits, at Ilford were being checked regularly for fossils by amateur scientists. Ilford is today a London suburb, but during the nineteenth century it was a village in Essex. Brickearth was dug out and turned into the bricks needed to build the railway which ran from London to the market town of Romford and also for the houses for people living in the village, as it expanded and underwent the transformation from Essex village to London suburb. Two things were immediately apparent during these fossil-hunting expeditions. The first was that the remains were regularly found of animals which no longer lived in Britain. Some, such as elephants, still lived in other parts of the world; others, such as the giant deer megaloceros, were extinct. No deer in the world had antlers which spanned ten feet. The other thing which was noticeable was that a cross-section through the pits being dug, showed that the land itself had changed dramatically since the deposits had been laid down. In the *Transactions of the Essex Field Club* for 1880 was a paper which perfectly illustrated this aspect of the matter. It was a lecture delivered by a man called Henry Walker and its humorous title was 'A Day's Elephant Hunting in Essex'. After describing how he and a party of men descended into a brick-pit, Walker said: 'It now begins to dawn on the uninitiated in our party that elephant hunting in Essex, in these modern days, is an underground sport – a recreation restricted to the subterranean world and no longer carried out in the open.' When they reached the bottom of the pit which had yielded up so many bones and fossils, Walker and the others found that they were looking at a vertical wall; a cross-section cut through the ground. As Walker said: 'A perpendicular face of the river-bed faces us some seventeen feet in height. Running from left to right until they disappear into the unexcavated ground, and pass away beneath modern Ilford, are horizontal bands of different coloured earths. These successive layers of loam and sand and gravel represent successive changes in the sediments brought down by the old and now vanished river which once flowed over the spot. In fact, we have a lesson here as to *how land is made.*'

During his lecture, Walker discussed the interesting fact that species at home in both cool and warm climates had been found in the brick fields: beavers and wolves, together with elephants and lions. He concluded that this was a consequence of two factors; a retreating ice sheet and also the rising of the land mass which cut Britain off from the mainland. In other words, he stated plainly that the evidence strongly suggested that the traditional view of the Earth as timeless, stable and unchanging was false and that species came and went. Some moved to other areas, while others became extinct. It was obvious that all this activity must have taken place over many thousands of years and that the Biblical record was contradicted by geological evidence. Deposits of sand, in which were found sea shells, indicated that parts of the country had once lain at the bottom of the ocean. These deposits had taken a very long time to accumulate.

It is very unlikely that anybody would have bothered to dig down twenty feet below the topsoil on the outskirts of London, thus uncovering a perfect record of past activity in the area over millions of years, unless there had been a powerful reason for doing so. In short, the demand for bricks to build houses for the many new commuters had provided the impetus to reveal in detail part of the planet's history. The needs of commuters had thus, indirectly, given vivid confirmation of Darwin's theories.

While examination of the cross-sections revealed when suburban brick fields were excavated provided some evidence for the age of the earth and the changing nature of the land, the navvies working on the new railways were performing a similar service. During the construction of the first railway line to connect London with another city, the London & Birmingham line in 1833, those laying the line came to a seemingly insurmountable obstacle at Blisworth in Northamptonshire. For over a mile, a rocky outcrop blocked the way; too steep and high to cross and too wide to skirt around. The solution was simple and brutal. The obstruction would need to be blown apart with gunpowder and an artificial canyon created for the railway to pass along. Three thousand barrels of gunpowder were used and a million cubic yards of rock, soil and clay removed, making a deep cutting through the rock.

The making of the Blisworth Cutting left the various rock strata exposed in an even more vivid illustration of the passage of many thousands of years than that afforded by the Ilford brick pits. Towering cliffs on either side of the line displayed bright yellow, brown, orange and white stripes which showed where the successive geological eras had left their mark. It was not necessary to conduct amateur, archaeological expeditions to view this visual record of the Earth's past. It was clearly visible to any passenger travelling between London and Birmingham; a glaring refutation of Bishop Ussher's carefully-planned 6,000-year history of creation. Anybody travelling through Blisworth Cutting could see at a glance that the earth had been going for longer than that!

With the thousands of new houses being built on the outskirts of Britain's cities, it was becoming increasingly impractical for all those living in the suburbs and working in the city to walk to their shops and offices each morning and then return home in the same way during the evening. Those with money could hire Hackney carriages, of course, or sometimes travel on a short-stage coach. The very rich, as had been the case for centuries, could run their own carriages. For the rest, urban travel was an increasingly tricky problem which began to be solved in the 1820s by the introduction of buses.

Since trains and cars are today common modes of travel for commuters and because there were no petrol-driven motor cars in the first half of the nineteenth century, it would be a reasonable guess that most commuters in Victorian Britain would have travelled by train. This might seem a logical conclusion, but it would be quite wrong. There were during the 1850s estimated to be a little over a quarter of a million commuters in London. A mere 27,000, just 10 per cent, travelled daily by train. The rest walked or used buses. It was widely noted that many working-class people never used trains at all. Before we examine the bus as the favoured means of commuting in Victorian Britain, as the lifestyle grew more popular, it is intriguing to look at a world of commuting which never really developed, although for a few years it looked as though it might have been the way of the future. We have already seen one urban vision which was toyed with and came to nothing, the idea of railway viaducts as pleasant boulevards and housing projects, rather than the urban blight which in fact they invariably became during that time. Perhaps a little diversion now might show us another possible course of history, in which powered buses and coaches became the principle means of commuting long before the invention of the internal combustion engine.

We tend today to assume that while the steam engine ruled the railways of Victorian Britain and powered ships on the high seas; the roads were destined inevitably to be dominated by horse-drawn transport. As a matter of fact, this was far from being a forgone conclusion in the early years of Victoria's reign and for a decade or so, it seemed that steam-driven, passenger-carrying vehicles would soon become a common sight on the country's roads and in the streets of the towns and cities. We shall look shortly at the way that the bus actually did become such a popular means of transport for commuters, but first we might look at some early buses of a most unusual type which were carrying commuters during the reign of William IV in the 1820s.

Goldsworthy Gurney was an archetypal gentleman-scientist of the early nineteenth century. He was a surgeon, architect, chemist and inventor all rolled into one. One of his inventions was a stagecoach which was driven by a steam engine and intended to be used not on rails, but on ordinary roads.

The prototype was developed in a workshop near London's Regent's Park in 1825 and 1826. It was driven to Hampstead Heath, Highgate and even further afield to Barnet, a village north of London. The vehicle reached speeds of 20 miles per hour on these test runs and as a result, Gurney decided to set up a regular service, which ran for some months between the cities of Cheltenham and Gloucester in the West of England. Three of Gurney's steam-driven vehicles were used and the service ran four times a day. There is some reason to suppose that businessmen travelling between the two cities used Gurney's new service to commute. The coaches used for the service between Cheltenham and Gloucester were extraordinarily sophisticated for their time. They foreshadowed many of the mechanical features which would not be seen again until motor cars made their appearance sixty years later. Speed-changing gears, compensating steering geometry and differential drive hubs were all to be found on the Gurney steam carriages.

Powerful interests were at work, however, to prevent steam carriages becoming successful on the roads. Companies running stagecoach services and others whose business relied upon horses felt threatened by this strange new means of transport. Together, these vested interests managed to push legislation through Parliament which placed a prohibitively high tariff on steam carriages. Ordinary horse-drawn stagecoaches had to pay a toll of two shillings (10p) a journey, while that for steam driven vehicles was set at £2, twenty times as high. Little wonder that the venture collapsed after only a short time.

But this was not to be the end of steam-powered buses and coaches. In 1833 Walter Hancock set up the London and Paddington Steam Carriage Company, with the aim of providing a fast and reliable commuter service from the well-to-do village of Paddington to the City of London. He previously experimented with running a service from Stratford in East London to the City of London; using a ten-seater bus called *Infant*. He did not have a license to carry paying passengers on this route, which was in the nature of a series of trial runs.

On 22 April 1833, Hancock's steam bus *Enterprise* began taking passengers from Paddington to the City. Later, the oddly-named *Autopsy* also went into service. Over the next three-and-a-half years, Hancock's buses carried 12,761 commuters to the City and back, travelling over 4,299 route miles in the process. Other companies followed Gurney and Hancock's lead, all catering for the commuter market. In the north of England, the London, Holyhead and Liverpool Steam Coach and Road Company began operating, with the intention of building new roads to cope with the demands of steam coaches, while the Steam Carriage Company of Scotland was running hourly services between Glasgow and Paisley. This too was aimed at commuters.

The opposition from traditional coaching companies, combined with the pressure that these businesses were able to exert on the Turnpike Trusts which maintained the roads, meant that these early 'horseless carriages' were probably doomed from the start. Walter Hancock's final commuter bus, the *Automaton*, is shown in Illustration 8. It stopped running in 1840. By that time, horse-drawn buses were becoming a common sight on the streets of London and other big cities. Most people are innately conservative about radical new developments and horses were a more comfortable and reassuring sight than a mechanical vehicle belching smoke and steam. It is interesting to wonder how suburban streets might have looked as the century drew on, if such machines had become widespread. There was no inherent reason why the steam transport of passengers by rail, rather than road, should have flourished and yet by about 1840, the die was cast. The roads of Britain would remain the preserve of horse-drawn vehicles and steam power would be restricted to the railways.

Curiously, the very first commuters to be brought in and out of London by steam power travelled neither by road or rail. It is sometimes forgotten that the River Thames itself functioned as a highway and that travelling along the river could be a good deal faster than using the roads. For this reason, some of the first regular commuters to central London were being brought to work by steam power before the Battle of Waterloo. In June 1814, the paddle steamer *Margery* was launched in the Scottish town of Dumbarton. For some months, the vessel plied the River Clyde, before being bought by the London-based firm of Cortis & Co. She was then sailed down the east coast of Britain and along the Thames Estuary to Gravesend, twenty miles or so downstream from London. On 23 January 1815, the *Margery* began a regular service to and from London. Businessmen living in Gravesend travelled to work by paddle steamer as soon as the ferry service began. Later that year, the *Duke of Argyll*, another Scottish boat, began a service between Margate and London, which also called at Gravesend.

By 1835, three steamship companies were running vessels along the River Thames, one of them, the Diamond Steam Packet Company, reporting that it carried a quarter of a million passengers that year. Not all of the passengers on these paddle steamers were commuters, of course. Gravesend and Margate were popular places for a day out for London tourists, but there is no doubt that a substantial number of those being ferried between Gravesend and London *were* commuters and that commuting of this sort predated the establishment of London buses or trains by fifteen years.

Before looking at the spread of horse-drawn buses and the way in which they became for some decades the mainstay of commuters, the next chapter will examine our perceptions of commuters through their representation in fiction. Ideas about commuting have changed in the last fifty years or so and whereas at one time an existence consisting of a little house in the suburbs and daily commuting to the office was viewed as a splendid lifestyle, it is now seen by many people as something akin to a prison sentence; a fate to be avoided, rather than embraced. This trend may be very clearly seen in the portrayal of commuters in novels, films and television programmes.

Chapter 3

From Bob Cratchit to Reginald Perrin: The Commuter in Fiction

S ome British place names seem to be inherently amusing. Take the seaside resort of Cleethorpes in the north of England, for example. A comedian need only mention 'Cleethorpes' or the neighbouring town of Grimsby in order to have an audience smiling in anticipation. Claiming that some formerly successful singer is now performing in an end-of-the-pier show in Cleethorpes is guaranteed to raise a laugh. The Surrey town of Surbiton suffers from this same syndrome; the name of the town itself sounding faintly ridiculous. 'Surbiton' suggests an association with suburban commuters and their lifestyle, which is why some locals call the town 'Suburbiton'. It was perhaps inevitable that when the BBC wished to make *The Good Life*, a situation comedy centred around commuters and former commuters, they should have set it in Surbiton.

Just as some places bring a smile to our lips almost automatically, so too do some lifestyles and types of character. The hen-pecked husband, for instance, or the aging rake. One such amusing stock character has, since the middle of the nineteenth century, been the commuter. It is a very curious thing that commuters are often seen as being a particular type of person; respectable, law-abiding, reliable, a little stuffy perhaps and definitely a creature of habit, catching exactly the same train each day. One is reminded of the theme song from the television comedy *Dad's Army*. We are told in *Who do You Think you are Kidding Mr Hitler* that, 'Mr Brown goes off to town on the 8:21'. This precision to the minute of a train's time of departure pretty well sums up how many of us see commuters. The commuter is a creature of habit and catches the same train at the same time every day.

In addition to being law-abiding and reliable, regular in their habits and perhaps a little humourless, with a tendency to take themselves seriously, what else can we say about the image of the archetypal commuter? Essentially, commuters are all too often viewed as being minor figures, little cogs in a big machine, one might say. This is odd, because of course among all those millions of commuters are Cabinet members, managing directors of international companies, senior civil servants and all manner of other significant people. In fact the most important individuals in the life of the nation are more likely than not to be commuters. Nevertheless, for the last 150 years or so, commuters have been regarded as being fictional fall guys; people whose role in novels, plays, films and television series is merely to amuse us by their lifestyle. This image is rooted in the fiction of the late nineteenth century, which more or less defined how commuters have been viewed by the rest of us ever since. It might also be mentioned at this point that for most of us, a typical commuter will be an office worker, rather than an artisan, a member of the middle, rather than the working, class. This is strange, because as we shall see, manual workers made up a very large proportion of commuters during the nineteenth century; just as they do today. Nevertheless, it is a fact that the word 'commuter' evokes images of clerks, rather than carpenters or electricians.

In Chapter 1, we met Bob Cratchit; a commuter from Dickens' most amusing and lighthearted work. Dickens had a fondness for commuters and worked them into a number of his books; creating some of the most familiar characters in Victorian fiction as he did so. All were, if not actually comic, then at least slightly ridiculous. Perhaps the most famous of all Dickens' commuters is to be found in *David Copperfield*. Wilkins Micawber, always waiting for something to turn up, was a feckless optimist. He was based upon Charles Dickens' own ineffectual father. Mr Micawber worked on commission for the company of Murdstone and Grinby, who had their offices and warehouse down on the River Thames at Blackfriars. Nominally, Micawber and his family were members of the middle class though and so lived away from central London at Windsor Terrace, off the City Road. Their gentility was only a façade, as they owed money to various tradesmen. Although desperately poor, they had an entire house to themselves, which, being in a suburb, lent them more status than money alone would do.

Mr Micawber lived in a 'walking suburb', as did another of Dickens' commuters. Wemmick, Mr Jaggers' clerk, is one of the most memorable characters from *Great Expectations*. He lived in Walworth, across the Thames from the office where he worked, which stood in the shadow of St Paul's Cathedral. With his constant references to the desirability of acquiring 'portable property', Wemmick acts as a light relief to the fearsome Jaggers. He walked home to South London each day to an eccentric little house built like a castle and surrounded by a moat. Like Tom and Barbara in *The Good Life*, Wemmick was a believer in the virtues of self-sufficiency. In his little suburban garden, he kept rabbits, chickens and a pig, as well as growing cucumbers and other vegetables. It is by no means impossible that Wemmick's curious little estate was in fact the inspiration for the television comedy.

Dickens' commuters are figures of fun, but also have a serious side; they are not complete clowns. All of them are minor characters in the novels in which they feature. Towards the end of the century though, as the walking suburbs gave way to areas where public transport was necessary to get to work in the morning, commuters became the protagonists of some of the great comic novels of the Victorian Era. Three books in particular served to establish the archetype of this sort of office worker.

In the summer of 1882, a novel was published in London by Smith, Elder & Co. It was written by Thomas Anstey Guthrie, using the pseudonym F. Anstey and it detailed the fantastic and humbling adventures of a solid and respectable commuter. Paul Bultitude is a successful businessman in his fifties, who runs an office in Mincing Lane in the City of London, a stone's-throw from the Tower of London and the Bank of England. His home is in Westbourne Terrace, in Bayswater. At once, we notice a difference between Mr Bultitude and the commuters found in Dickens' novels. Mr Micawber lives only a mile and a half from his place of work, while Bob Cratchit and Wemmick both have their homes a couple of miles from their offices in the city, in Camden and Walworth respectively. All three lived in 'walking suburbs'. Paul Bultitude, on the other hand, has a house which is five miles from his office. It would scarcely have been practical for him to have walked home each evening from Mincing Lane to Bayswater. We know from the text that he travels to and from the office sometimes by Hansom cab or, on other occasions, by using the Underground to Praed Street; a station on the Metropolitan Railway which ran from Moorgate.

As a consequence of a plot device involving a magic talisman, Mr Bultitude swaps bodies with his thirteen-year-old son and ends up going off to boarding school in his son's place. The humour of *Vice Versa* centres around the supposed character of a typical commuter of the time. Mr Bultitude is pompous, humourless and a creature of habit. He lives a comfortable life, largely defined by his work and social position. It is his inability to adapt to his changed circumstances which provides the laughs. The book works chiefly because readers would be expected to see a protagonist who was a commuter as somebody who already possessed comic potential. Watching the staid, hidebound and meticulous City businessman trying to survive in conditions vastly different from those to which he is accustomed made the book a minor masterpiece.

Vice Versa hinged then upon one aspect of the popular view of the commuter in late Victorian Britain, that of a man who was such a creature of habit that he was quite unable to adapt to any sudden and abrupt change in routine. A book published seven years later, and still enormously popular to this day, made brief mention of an episode in the life of another commuter and in doing so touched upon another of the characteristics which defined the typical commuter; the obsession with punctuality. This needs a little explanation. Before the Industrial Revolution, the rhythm of the working day was largely regulated by the rising and the setting of the sun. With industrialisation came a new pattern of working habits; one dictated by the necessity of men and women arriving at factories for shifts which began at a set time each day, whatever the season. Those arriving late might be docked half a day's pay, even for turning up only ten or fifteen minutes past their allotted starting time. This same routine of punctuality became established also in the counting houses and offices employing the vast army of commercial clerks needed to keep the wheels of industry turning smoothly and efficiently.

In *Three Men in a Boat*, Jerome K. Jerome gives us a brief glimpse of an incident in the life of George; one of the eponymous central characters of the book. George works at a bank in the City of London and one night forgets to wind his watch. He wakes up in the middle of the night and because his watch has stopped at 8:20, he concludes that this is the time; although it is really a little before three in the morning. Hurrying through the streets to catch his bus, George is in a panic because he must be at his office by nine. This frantic fear of being late for work is another of those features of the archetype which we associate with the commuter. Jerome K. Jerome's most famous book is undoubtedly *Three Men in a Boat*, but he wrote a sequel, which is not nearly so well known. *Three Men on the Bummel* tells the story of the same three men from the earlier book; this time on a cycling holiday through Germany. It contains a marvellous portrait of a commuter, one desperately anxious not to miss his train in the morning.

Being a minute or two late for work in a factory was one thing, but a minute's difference arriving at the station when commuting by train could make one half an hour late in getting to the office. This was because the trains left at a precise time, and having missed one, there was no choice but to wait for the next. For this reason, getting to the station on time in the morning became a matter of the greatest importance to commuters. With more and more people depending on public transport to get them to work, it became vital to know the time to the very minute. It has even been suggested that the White Rabbit in *Alice's Adventures in Wonderland* is based upon the harried commuter rushing for his train in the morning. Readers will recall that he takes out a pocket watch and, after consulting it, declares, 'Oh dear! Oh dear! I shall be too late!' When next Alice catches up with him, the rabbit is still fretting about the time, saying, 'Oh my ears and whiskers, how late it's getting!'

Even when commuters were walking to work, there was still a frantic desire to avoid being late and an almost obsessive interest by some employers in catching them out at their tardiness. This is to be seen in the very first fictional commuter, Bob Cratchit. On the day after Christmas Day, Cratchit is due in at the office. The reformed Ebenezer Scrooge is waiting for him and, in a reversion to his old ways, notes exactly how late his clerk is: 'The clock struck nine. No Bob. A quarter past. No Bob. He was a full eighteen minutes and a half behind his time.' In fiction, as in real life, timekeeping by commuters was measured in fractions of a minute throughout the whole of Victoria's reign.

Returning now to Jerome K. Jerome's novel, *Three Men on the Bummel*, which was first published in 1900. By this time, commuters were able to live even further from the city than Mr Bultitude in *Vice Versa*. Uncle Podger, vividly described by Jerome in *Three Men in a Boat*, is revealed to be a commuter living in Ealing. This West London district is over ten miles from the City of London, making transport of some kind essential. We are told that, 'Many stout City gentlemen lived at Ealing in those days . . . and caught early trains to Town.' Uncle Podger 'would start from Ealing Common by the nine-thirteen train to Moorgate Street'. There follows a detailed account of how Uncle Podger and various other commuters never leave enough time to get to the station to catch the train, but always end up running across Ealing Common in a frantic dash to catch the train to Town. Each man has a newspaper and black bag in one hand and an umbrella in the other: 'It was not a showy spectacle. They did not run well, they did not even run fast; but they were earnest, and they did their best. The exhibition appealed less to one's sense of art than to one's natural admiration for conscientious effort.'

The books so far mentioned contain characters who are commuters, although commuting itself is only incidental to their plots. We come now to a nineteenth-century classic which is entirely about commuting and the domestic life of an ordinary and unremarkable commuter. It is a book described by Evelyn Waugh as 'the funniest book in the world' and which J. B. Priestly regarded as being 'immortal' and a 'masterpiece'. George and Weedon Grossmith's *The Diary of a Nobody* first appeared as a weekly column in *Punch*, the humorous magazine. It proved so popular that in 1892 it was published as a book.

The Diary of a Nobody is a fictionalised, first-person account of the life and times of a commercial clerk living in a London suburb. Mr Pooter has, over the years, come to symbolise the middle-class British commuter who works in an office. He shares a number of features with other fictional commuters at whom we have looked. For example, he is punctual and reliable to an almost fanatical degree. Any failure in this respect is seen by the narrator as being a serious matter: 'Today was a day of annoyances. I missed the quarter-to-nine 'bus to the City, through having words with the grocer's boy . . .' As a result of this misfortune, 'I was half-an-hour late at the office, a thing that has never happened to me before'.

Mr Pooter is also conventional, pompous and slightly ridiculous, qualities which have been observed in the other commuters from the pages of Victorian novels. There is more to this individual than just that, though. He is also loyal, industrious, law-abiding and reliable. He is in fact the ideal worker, who assures the head of the firm for which he works, when terrible trouble threatens the business, 'Mr Perkupp, I will work day and night to serve you!' For over twenty years, Mr Pooter has worked for the same firm, and has never once taken a day off through illness. As he tells his son, upon being given an unexpected pay-rise: 'My boy, as a result of twenty-one years industry and strict attention to the interests of my superiors in office, I have been rewarded with promotion and a rise in salary of £100.' The life of this most famous of commuters revolves almost entirely around his job; the duties of which, he undertakes with an attitude approaching reverence.

The life of Mr Pooter is inextricably bound up with the lifestyle of commuting. In the first paragraph, it is stated that the new house to which the Pooters have just moved is in Brickfield Terrace, Holloway. Although it is today regarded as being an inner-city area, in the late nineteenth century, Holloway was one of the newer suburbs, whose houses had only recently been built. The name of the street, Brickfield Terrace, is a joke as well. The bricks from which London suburbs were constructed, were of course dug from vast brickfields and fired in nearby kilns. Illustration 6 shows such a kiln which has somehow survived in Notting Hill. After the brickfields had been thoroughly excavated, houses were built over them. A street constructed over such an abandoned site might very aptly be named Brickfield Terrace.

Commuter transport is an integral part of the life explored in *The Diary of a Nobody*. Again, we do not get past the first paragraph of the book before discovering that there is, 'a nice little back garden which runs down to the railway'. Later on, we find that the road in which the Pooters live is a bus route: 'Hearing my 'bus pass the window, I was obliged to rush out of the house . . .'. Like many lower middle-class commuters, Mr Pooter wished to make his home stylish and sophisticated. In Illustration 9, we see him hanging up a stag's head made of plaster-of-paris and painted brown, on the grounds that this, 'will look just the thing for our little hall and give it style'. This was parodied in the television comedy *Fawlty Towers*, when Basil Fawlty puts a moose's head up in the lobby, on the same grounds; that it will add 'style'.

We shall look next at the sea change which the depiction of fictional commuters underwent after the end of the Second World War, but we cannot leave the subject of Victorian commuters without looking at a fairly insignificant example of the breed whose sole claim to fame is appearing as a corpse in the only Sherlock Holmes story to involve the London Underground. Cadogan West is a young clerk at the Woolwich Arsenal, who commutes to work each day, working nine to five in an office. He lives with his mother on the outskirts of London and travels to Woolwich by train.

The Bruce-Partington Plans, from *His Last Bow*, introduces the mystery of Cadogan West's body being discovered by the tracks of the Underground near Aldgate Station. In his pocket are some important documents relating to a revolutionary kind of submarine. The mystery is of course, how he came to be laying by the railway tracks. Did he fall from a train and if so, how? There is a detailed description of the line near Aldgate, as well as discussions about ticket collectors and various other aspects of travelling by Underground at the turn of the century. The case is in the end solved by Holmes working out that the body of the unfortunate young commuter must have been laying on the roof of a train and been tipped off by the centrifugal force as a bend was rounded. Cadogan West is thus shown to be not a treacherous spy, as was suspected, but rather a victim of murder.

The image of the commuter as being a steady, industrious, conventional sort of soul, dedicated to the interests of his employer, was to undergo something of a change in twentieth-century depictions of the breed on television and in films. In Dickens' novels, commuters are used as a counterbalance to more serious characters. Mr Micawber provides light relief from the horrors of Murdstone and Grinby's warehouse, Bob Cratchit is an amusing contrast to Ebenezer Scrooge, and Wemmick acts as a foil to Jaggers the lawyer. Later on, the commuter develops into a faintly comic type who lives for his work. Mr Pooter is one such and although we laugh at him, we are also keenly aware of his sterling worth. He is sober and sensible, taking his job seriously and finding comfort in the regular habits associated with commuting. By the beginning of the 1960s, the traditional view of the fictional commuter was beginning to alter. We can see this transformation clearly in the 1961 film, *The Rebel*.

In *The Rebel*, Tony Hancock is almost a caricature of the commuter. He religiously catches the same train each morning to the office where he works. He wears a suit and a bowler hat, and carries a copy of *The Times* under his arm. His work, poring over ledgers in an office along with a dozen identical clerks, is an updated version of Mr Pooter's workplace. Times have changed, though, and whereas for the commercial clerks of Victorian Britain, the commuting lifestyle was a reassuring routine which spelled security and safety from the spectre of poverty, to Tony Hancock it is a wearisome straitjacket. He longs to escape from the daily grind of commuting and it is this fierce desire to be free of the restrictions of this life that turns him into the rebel of the film's title, and leads to various adventures. He moves to Paris and becomes an abstract artist. This film captured perfectly the mood of the time. During the 1950s, playwright John Osborne gave us the 'Angry Young Man', who despises staid, bourgeois society. Suburban life was anathema to such people. Interestingly enough, in *The Rebel*, John le Mesurier refers to the clerks in the office where Tony Hancock works as 'Angry young men'.

This idea, that commuting was something to break free of if humanly possible, gathered pace during the 1960s. It was all bound up with a distaste for the suburbs and anything associated with them. The respectable commuter who was dissatisfied with his life and sought adventure, became a clichéd figure in such television programmes as *Monty Python's Flying Circus*. In one sketch, a chartered accountant visits a vocational guidance counsellor, because he wishes for a job that gives his life new meaning. The counsellor tells him that the character profile produced from the questionnaires which he has filled out, indicate that he is timid, dull and lacking a sense of humour. It is understood that this man is a typical, dreary commuter and that he has a burning desire to break out of the mould. His declared intention is to become a lion tamer! The humour here is essentially that of *The Rebel*. Commuting is a soul–destroying lifestyle and those trapped in it sometimes wish to break free.

It was *Monty Python's Flying Circus* which popularised the idea of the commuter towns of Surbiton and Purley as places fit only to be scorned, at the same time that the magazine *Private Eye* was turning the London district of Neasden into a laughing stock. A year after the last series of *Monty Python's Flying Circus* ended in 1974, the BBC screened a new situation comedy called *The Good Life*. It tells the story of a disillusioned commuter called Tom Good, who lives in Surbiton. On his fortieth birthday, he realises that there must be more to life than the daily commute to the office. Just like the offices shown in *The Diary of a Nobody* and *The Rebel*, Tom Good's office in *The Good Life* is a dull and uninviting place. The work which he carries out there is depressing and pointless; he designs plastic animals to be given away in packets of breakfast cereal. Like Tony Hancock and the would–be lion tamer in *Monty Python*, the protagonist of *The Good Life* suffers an existential crisis and decides that there must be more to life than commuting and working in an office. He and his wife come to the decision that they will set up a farm in the garden of their Surbiton home and become self–sufficient.

It was perhaps inevitable that it would be Surbiton in which this Tolstoyan experiment should be launched by a commuter and his wife. The Goods' neighbour continues to commute to work to the same firm that Tom was formerly employed by. Much of the humour of the programme hinges around the supposed sterility and pointlessness of the lives of the couple living next door to the Goods, who are unable to break away from what is portrayed as a dreary existence of dull conformity. All the audience's sympathy is intended to be with those who reject the life of the suburban commuter.

The same year that *The Good Life* began to be broadcast, a novel was published which touched upon a similar theme – the despair of a commuter trapped in a meaningless existence. This too was a humorous treatment of the subject. In *The Death of Reginald Perrin*, David Nobbs gives us a commuter whose life is empty and boring. Like Tom Good, this is a man who is undergoing a mid-life crisis. The novel was swiftly adapted for television, first being broadcast under the title *The Fall and Rise of Reginald Perrin* in the autumn of 1976.

Reginald Perrin lives in the fictional London district of Climthorpe. There is reason to suppose that Climthorpe is really none other than a thinly-disguised Surbiton. One of the ways that Reginald Perrin's mental disintegration is charted and measured is by his increasingly late arrival at work. As we saw above, punctuality is one of the chief distinguishing features of the true commuter and the way in which Reginald Perrin is first eleven minutes late for work, then seventeen and twenty-two minutes late, tells us clearly that he has stopped caring about his job at Sunshine Desserts. The excuses produced by the protagonist for his dilatoriness become more and more bizarre. On one occasion, he blames a defective junction box at New Malden. Assuming that Reginald Perrin works in London, then a rail journey from Surbiton would take him straight through New Malden.

We might pause here and consider once more the extraordinary change in perspective which took place between fictional commuters in the later twentieth centuries, compared with those at whom we looked from a century earlier. Reginald Perrin and Tom Good were middle-aged men, desperate at all costs to break free of what they saw as the constricting life style of commuting to and from the suburbs. Looking back again at Mr Pooter from *The Diary of a Nobody,* we are able to see that his own views on this subject were diametrically opposed in every way to those of the more modern commuters from television and film. Far from wishing to escape from the suburbs, Mr Pooter is passionately attached to them and would regard being forced out of the suburbs as a tragedy on a par with the expulsion from Eden! Having saved his employer's business by his phenomenal loyalty, his boss asks him, 'Do you like your house and are you happy where you are?' Mr Pooter's reply to this question underlines the radical change in attitude at which we have been looking. He says, 'Yes sir; I love my house and I love the neighbourhood, and could not bear to leave it.' Of course, we must not lose sight of the fact that both the Goods and Mr Pooter are fictional commuters and not real people. Nevertheless, they were neither of them created in vacuums and are reflections of the enormous difference in perceptions of what constitutes a satisfying and fulfilling life. Most people today would perhaps tend to sympathise with the views of Reginald Perrin and Tom Good towards suburban life and the commuting lifestyle, rather than Mr Pooter's.

Commuters no longer seem to be such a ready target for humour these days. It is, at any rate, some years since anybody thought it worth making them the focal point of any sort of drama, humorous or otherwise. Digs at commuters these days tend to be indirect, often using places associated with commuters, rather than they themselves to make a point. Surbiton, the epitome of a commuter town, is still used from time to time as a shorthand way of denoting what is thought to be the typical commuter mind-set of being a little reactionary in viewpoint. The soap opera *EastEnders* wished to indicate that a black woman had found life difficult growing up as a child, having been adopted by white parents and raised in a white area. Ava Hartman, in the episode of *EastEnders* broadcast on 23 November 2012, was given the perfect childhood home to illustrate and underline the problems which she encountered in early life, by explaining that she had been brought up in Surbiton. No more needed to be said on the subject; mention of Surbiton told viewers all that they needed to know. Poor woman!

Another location near London which has come to epitomise commuting and life in the suburbs is the south London district of Purley, which lies to the south of Croydon. Purley was mentioned in several sketches on *Monty Python's Flying Circus,* and viewers were given to understand that it was a deadly dull place full of commuters. Although *Monty Python* was in the habit of mocking commuters and suburbia, not all television producers saw the lifestyle of commuting in such terms; as something to be sneered at. Just as with *The Diary of a Nobody* there was, side by side with the feeling that commuters were ridiculous, the idea that there was also something solid and praiseworthy about those living in the suburbs like Mr Pooter and working loyally for a firm in the City. So it was that in 1979, a BBC situation comedy began, which showed a commuter and his wife moving into their new house in Poplar Avenue in Purley. From the beginning, there was something about *Terry and June* which appealed to ordinary viewers. They were not laughing *at* the Medfords, but *with* them at themselves. The humour of *Terry and June* was utterly innocuous and generated laughs without any of the innuendo and smut which was beginning to be such a regular feature of other television comedies at that time. Families could sit together and watch *Terry and June* without needing to have the slightest apprehension that they would be made to feel embarrassed about any of the jokes.

The humour of *Terry and June* was very similar to that found in *The Diary of a Nobody*. Like Mr Pooter, Terry Medford is a commuter and lives a dull, blameless life. Nothing in particular happens to him or his wife and any laughter comes as a natural consequence of everyday life in a suburban, middle-class home. There is never any anger or unpleasantness and each episode leaves the viewer feeling that this must be a good life to lead. Neither Terry nor June suffer from any angst about the pointlessness of their existence or anything of that kind. A typical plot line involves Terry not wishing to admit to his superior at the office that he is unable to play bridge. Admittedly, this would be something of a *faux pas* in such an obviously respectable middle-class man living in Purley and we sympathise with his social embarrassment. It is his solution to the problem which is amusing; he decides that he and his wife should master the game of bridge to a high level in the course of a single weekend, so that he can play with his boss and her wife when they visit.

Purley still maintains its reputation as a slightly peculiar suburb, whose residents fret about the kind of things that the rest of the country takes for granted. At the time of writing, for example, its inhabitants are much exercised by plans to build a 'skyscraper' in their beloved district. On closer examination, this building turns out not to be a skyscraper in any usual meaning of the word, but rather a sixteen-story residential block of flats. The proposed development has however been enough to unite over 93 per cent of those living in Purley against it.

The decline of the commuter as a figure of fun is due in part to the fact that it is no longer possible to point to a particular type and identify the person infallibly as being a commuter. Anybody standing outside a Tube station in the City of London will wait in vain to spot any signs that this or that passenger stepping off the escalator is definitely a commuter. The days are long past when one could see at a glance the bowler hat and umbrella of the 'City gent'. Commuters today come in all shapes, sizes and shades and have no readily apparent external signals of their status. This means that the commuter is on the verge of extinction as a stock character with a typical appearance and predictable mentality.

The lack of an easily recognisable visual image which viewers would immediately identify as being a commuter, has had a deleterious effect upon cartoonists. Until as late as the 1980s, the magazine *Punch* would regularly feature cartoons about commuters, these being calculated to appeal to their overwhelmingly middle-class readership, many of whom were themselves commuters. Often, these men, for in cartoons, commuters were invariably male, were shown standing on the platform of a railway station or perhaps sitting in a compartment on a train. In such a case, there was little need to worry unduly about giving them a detailed appearance. The very fact that they were travelling by railway, suggesting at once that they were commuters. Often, the humour in such situations centres around the snobbishness of the dyed-in-the-wool commuter. One of David Langdon's cartoons from the 1970s shows two elderly-looking men in a first class railway compartment discussing a younger man, who is sitting some distance from them. One of the older men is saying to the other, 'On "Good Morning" terms until I discovered that he was a junior executive at BR with a free travel warrant'. Obviously, these men are *bona fide* season ticket holders and feel that they have been tricked into familiarity with a social inferior. There was no need at all for Langdon to draw anything in the way of clothing, other than a few vague, black smudges; these men could only be commuters.

When a cartoon, from *Punch* or the *Evening Standard*, wished to indicate that a man was a commuter, without including any of the defining backgrounds such as stations or trains; the convention was simple and straightforward. All that was required were pinstripe trousers, a bowler hat and umbrella, and hey presto, everybody knew that this was a commuter. Although this image of the commuter as having the appearance of a stockbroker or barrister was growing threadbare by the 1970s, it lingered on in the public's perception and long after one might reasonably expect to encounter anybody wearing a bowler hat on the streets of the City of London, the bowler-hatted commuter lived on in the pages of magazines and newspapers.

The perfect example of the commuter in cartoons is of course Bristow, who appeared in the London *Evening Standard* every day for forty years. Bristow is a clerk in the buying department of the Chester Perry organisation. He is a middle-aged commuter, who travels into Town each day from East Winchley. Bristow, drawn by Frank Dickens, first appeared in the *Aberdeen Press & Journal* In 1961 and ran continuously in that newspaper until 2012, making it, according to the *Guinness Book of Records*, the world's longest-running daily strip cartoon.

Inevitably, Bristow wears a dark jacket and pinstripe trousers. A bowler hat completes the archetype. One glance at him tells us at once that he is a commuter. Several of the common features at which we have been looking in this chapter may be found in Bristow. He is habitually late for work, for example, although this never seems to worry him unduly. Like so many fictional commuters since the war, Bristow began to appear in the same year that Tony Hancock's *The Rebel* was released, Bristow is frustrated and feels that he is capable of far more than just shuffling papers around in an office. At times, he dreams of being a brain surgeon, and he is also a budding author who has written a long novel called *Living Death in the Buying Department*. He is, alas, unable to find a publisher for this.

The recurring theme of the commuter being late for work has been a constant source of humour since the nineteenth century. Uncle Podger running across Ealing Common to catch his train, Reginald Perrin arriving at the office seventeen minutes late, Bristow often ends up signing the 'Late, late book'. Why actually should the lateness of fictional commuters be so amusing to us? The early nineteenth century essayist and philosopher William Hazlitt explains why the commuter arriving late at the office or running for a train which he might miss should tickle us so. He said: 'Man is the only animal that laughs and weeps; for he is the only animal that is struck with the difference between what things are, and what they ought to be.' Here we have the matter in a nutshell. We know that the genuine commuter is concerned about punctuality to an almost fanatical degree. When we see one who regularly arrives at the office late or who is so disorganised that he ends up running for the train every day, it is the dissonance between this and the way that we imagine a commuter *should* be, that is it say well-organised and always on time, which causes us to smile.

No account of fictional commuting, however brief, would be complete without at least some reference to the poetry of John Betjeman. The one line of Betjeman's poetry which everybody knows is of course, is that which begins the poem *Slough*; 'Come friendly bombs and fall on Slough'. Betjeman is widely regarded as being the arch-apostle of anti-modernism and an avowed opponent of all things suburban. This is odd, because he actually shows a great deal of affection for the lifestyle of the lower middle-class commuter. He may have been fond of rural scenes and Victorian architecture, but John Betjeman also had a distinct soft spot for the certain aspects of the modern world.

Betjeman's poems are full of imagery drawn straight from the modern, industrial world; with a particular emphasis on those standbys of commuter transport, the Tube, bus, tram and suburban railway train. Although sometimes expressing regret for the lost countryside which has been concreted over to provide homes for commuters, John Betjeman also displays affection for the comfortable, suburban life of the commuter. Here he is in *The Metropolitan Railway,* describing the mundane life of one such commuter, who lives in Ruislip and works in the City:

And all that day in murky London Wall,
The thought of RUISLIP kept him warm inside,

> At FARRINGDON that lunch hour at a stall,
> He bought a dozen plants of London Pride

It is unfortunate that the oft-quoted line about bombs falling on Slough has blinded us to Betjeman's affection for commuters and the suburbs in which they live. It is true that he is sometimes saddened by the contrast between the open countryside which he knew as a boy in Middlesex and Hertfordshire as when he talks in *Hertfordshire,* firstly of the

> Colour-washed cottages reed-thatched,
> And weather-boarded water mills,

before going on to contrast them with what is now to be found in that same part of the county;

> Tall concrete standards line the lane,
> Brick boxes glitter in the sun.

It is this kind of thing which has given casual readers the idea that John Betjeman abhorred suburban commuters and all their works! However, such negative references to commuters and their influence are greatly outweighed by the many cheerful descriptions to be found in his poetry of the Underground, as it spreads its tentacles out of London. Consider this, from *Middlesex*;

> Gaily into Ruislip Gardens,
> Runs the red electric train.

This too is a poem about a commuter. In this case, it is a young woman called Elaine, who;

> Hurries down the concrete station
> With a frown of concentration

before, later that evening, she

> Settles down to supper and the television screen.

Reading these wonderfully evocative verbal portraits of London commuters, one is struck by the way that John Betjeman demonstrates his liking and understanding of the modern world, just as he does of the rural past of which he writes so nostalgically. His sympathy for the commuter extends back into the past too; Mr and Mrs Pooter and their son feature in several of his more well-known poems. One is dedicated entirely to them. *Thoughts on 'The Diary of a Nobody'* is a reflection upon one episode from the book and works in a reference to a commuter train;

> And chuffs the Great Northern train
> For Alexandra Palace bound.

The Pooters are also mentioned in *Middlesex* and *In Willesden Churchyard*. The latter begins with the deliciously improbably lines, 'Come walk with me, my love, to Neasden Lane'.

This is by no means an exhaustive survey of literary manifestations of the British commuter, but even in the short sample at which we have looked, definite patterns emerge about the way that commuters have been viewed over the years. These patterns and changes reflect society as a whole, in which the commuters move and have their lives. The certainties of the Victorian Age of Empire tended to breed men who were content in their positions and assured of their good fortune in being in steady employment; men like Mr Pooter. The sense of entitlement lays heavily upon the pages of *The Diary of a Nobody*, with the Pooters and their friends having no doubt that theirs is the best possible life, in this, the best of all possible worlds.

By the time that the Second World War had drawn to a close fifty years later, both the physical and psychological world of the Pooters and their like had been smashed to atoms. Not only did the post-war generation in Britain not feel that same sense of satisfaction about the world which they inhabited, there was a tendency actively to reject and vilify it. The smug, self-satisfied commuter from suburbia symbolised all that was wrong about the old ways. Not only did the younger men and women of the late 1950s and early 1960s not feel that they were part of a stable and unchanging world; they had no wish to be so. Commuting tended to be lumped in with and regarded as being all of a piece with suburban life and both were rejected by the angry young men and their subsequent avatars in the 1970s and later.

Chapter 4

The Advent of the Omnibus: A Middle-Class Mode of Transport

The horse bus was the first popular method of commuting, apart that is from walking under one's own power. Like the steam carriages though, which preceded them, buses, or omnibuses to give them their full and correct name, were viewed at first with some suspicion. Even the name was thought to be vulgar.

The world's first buses, although they were not known as such, were eight-seater coaches operated by a company run by the French philosopher Blaise Pascal. These enjoyed something of a vogue in Paris during the late seventeenth century, even the King of France taking a trip by one. The novelty of this new method of transport wore off, though, and on Pascal's death, the enterprise folded. It was to be another 150 years before anybody else began operating urban buses. Once again, the location was Paris. In 1819, Jacques Lafitte set up a company which ran a fleet of buses throughout the French capital, each able to carry between sixteen and eighteen passengers.

It was not until four years after Jacques Lafitte began carrying passengers on what were in fact buses in all but name, that the expression 'omnibus' was coined. Stanislas Baudrey was the proprietor of Turkish Baths on the outskirts of the city of Nantes in western France. To promote his establishment, Baudrey began collecting customers from the centre of Nantes in covered coaches and, after bringing them to his baths, having them driven back again. He soon found that this part of his business, which began as a free service, was far more popular than his Turkish Baths. People living in the suburbs of Nantes were very glad to have a way of travelling into the centre of town and back in comfort. In time, he closed the baths and concentrated entirely upon providing a cheap and convenient transport service to and from the suburbs of Nantes.

Baudrey decided that he needed a catchy and original name for his public transport vehicles. Near the central terminus of his coaches was the shop of a hatter, one M. Omnes. Making an erudite play of words on his own name, which in Latin means 'all', Omnes had placed a sign over his shop window, bearing the legend 'Omnes Omnibus'. This translates freely as the somewhat boastful claim of 'all for all' or perhaps 'everything for all'. Baudrey knew enough Latin to realise that 'omnibus' could mean 'everything', but might equally well be translated as 'everybody'. It was the perfect name for the service which he was providing and so he promptly began calling his coaches 'omnibuses'.

The story of buses in Britain, which soon became such a boon for commuters, began on 5 April 1829, when a man who had at one time worked as a coach builder for Jacque Lafitte wrote to the London authority in charge of roads and vehicles travelling upon them, saying 'I am engaged in building two vehicles after the recently established French omnibus, which when completed I propose starting on the Paddington Road'. There was no objection to the experiment and so on 4 July 1829, George Shillibeer began the capital's first bus service; running between the Yorkshire Stingo, a pub in Paddington, and the Bank of England.

The omnibuses, which were at first more commonly known as 'Shillibeers', after their builder and operator, were promoted as being extremely respectable. This was important, because Shillibeer hoped to attract travellers who could afford to pay for the new service. The prices were high to begin with, a shilling (5p) for the whole journey or 6d (2½p) for any part of it. In order to make any sort of profit from the business, each bus would need to be full, which meant persuading those who could afford to travel in this way that it was a pretty stylish and desirable mode of transport. An advertisement emphasised this by claiming that, 'A person of great respectability attends each vehicle as conductor'. These, the first bus conductors in Britain, were the sons of naval officers and were dressed in uniforms designed to mimic those of a midshipman of the Royal Navy. Newspapers and magazines were provided so that the passengers could while away the time during their journey.

There were one or two features of the new system which, while familiar to us today, were revolutionary at the time. For instance, the buses would start at the given time regardless of how many people were in them. They could carry up to twenty-two passengers, but even if there were only one or two, the bus would start out for the City, just the same. The egalitarian nature of buses was also new. Anybody who could pay the fare was welcome aboard and this made them something of a social leveller. Some of those using them might be from the upper classes and other merely shopkeepers; all were equal on the omnibus. There was no first or second class travel. Perhaps the most radical part of the operation was that there was no need to book in advance and that all that was necessary was to turn up and board the bus as and when you required to travel.

From the first day of operation, commuters were the bread and butter of George Shillibeer's omnibuses. Paddington was a wealthy village near Bayswater and many of those living there were bankers and businessmen who had to get to the City each day. Obviously, at a shilling each way, only the very successful could afford to use these first omnibuses regularly. However, the laws of economics dictate that once there is widespread demand for some commodity or service, then men and women will come forward to supply it. The inevitable consequence of this will be that with increases in both demand and supply, the price will tend to fall, which is what duly happened with the new omnibuses of London. For the short length of time that he held a monopoly on buses, Shillibeer was raking in about £100 a day, but such fantastic sums could not last for long. Other people began to run their own omnibuses and before long there were almost 100 buses plying the route between Paddington and the City. Competition grew so stiff that Shillibeer renamed his vehicles, 'Shillibeer's Original Omnibuses' in order to distinguish them from the large number of, as he saw it, spurious omnibuses.

This free-for-all scramble for commuters wishing to travel between Paddington and the City could not last forever. All else apart, the customers themselves were beginning to complain about the races in which the bus drivers were engaged and the scrambles to persuade passengers to travel on this or that omnibus. At the height of this mad situation, there were almost 100 buses a day fighting for trade along the four-mile route. Eventually, a truce was agreed and the different operators agreed to set up an Omnibus Association. George Shillibeer was appointed Chairman of the new organisation. The number of buses running between Paddington and the City was reduced to fifty-seven, running at three-minute intervals throughout the day. Inspectors were employed to make sure that everybody abided by the new rules.

It wasn't long before new routes began to open up, chiefly towards the suburbs. Competition for the patronage of commuters was vigorous and indeed violent at times. On one particular route, that running between Putney and St. Paul's Cathedral, passengers often had an exciting time of it. When two or three companies were vying for custom, they would use any means to acquire passengers. If another company's bus was due to be at a stop at a certain time, then rivals would try and get there a few minutes earlier and persuade the waiting commuters that it would be quicker to travel with them instead. This resulted in races between buses, to see which could be the first to reach the next stop. These games turned into something like the chariot race from the film *Ben Hur*, with drivers trying to force rival vehicles to overturn at sharp bends. In time, the Omnibus Association succeeded in putting an end to these dangerous games, just as they had on the original bus route.

Useful as they were to commuters, there was from the first felt to be something a little vulgar about buses, a feeling which was particularly strong among those well-off enough not to need them. Those who could afford to run their own carriages or even others who were in the habit of taking Hackney Carriages hired in the street, objected to the roads becoming congested with the sometimes garishly painted coaches of the new companies. Even the name of the things was found to be offensive, especially when once the common abbreviation which is universally used today became the fashion.

Of course, nobody today talks of omnibuses, any more than they would call a pram a perambulator. In the case of omnibuses, it did not take all that long for cockneys to start shortening the name and referring to the bus, rather than the omnibus. This word then took off and soon came to replace the cumbersome 'omnibus'. There was just one problem and that was that 'bus' in popular usage already had a meaning. It referred to a particularly rough or even violent kiss. Having the same expression to mean the horse-drawn mode of transport might perhaps be a reference to the close proximity of the passengers to each other and the possibility that if the vehicle went over a bump, they might indeed find themselves 'bussing' one another. For whatever reason, the word 'bus' took some time to become polite usage and it was not until as late as 1935 that London Transport officially began using 'bus' in preference to 'omnibus'.

Shillibeer's omnibuses might have begun the commuter revolution, but it did George Shillibeer little good in the long run. He was unable to cope with the unexpectedly large number of rivals and in March 1831, less than two years after he launched his bus service, he was declared bankrupt. He found success later though as the inventor or a new type of hearse, the design of which was influenced by his previous experience in the field of public transport.

Buses were certainly an exciting novelty for the commuters of London, but to begin with they made little difference to the great mass of men and women who wished to get to work in the morning. A good weekly wage for a clerical worker in 1829 might have been a pound. Bearing in mind that the six-day week was the rule at that time and that Shillibeer's buses cost a shilling each way between Paddington and the City, would mean that that it would cost twelve shillings (60p) a week in fares to commute by bus. This would leave little of a clerk's pound a week actually to live on! Of course, as we saw, the fierce competition which began almost as soon as the Shillibeer omnibuses began running had the effect of bringing down prices and before long, the standard bus fare had halved. Even sixpence each way though was likely to take a large chunk of the average worker's wages. It was for this reason that Victorian buses were always a middle-class means of commuting. Both the cost and the fact that they did not begin running until eight in the morning, long after many manual workers were due at work, ensured that they remained that way.

Despite the steep cost of the new method of travel, buses quickly became so popular among commuters, that routes began springing up in all directions. By 1833, the rush hour had become a recognised feature of London life and somebody catching a bus home from a trip to town wrote about this unwelcome new phenomenon: 'Decent clerks, fagged and harmless, going home for their tea. Here we are, in all six and twenty sweating citizens, jammed, crammed and squeezed into each other like so many peas in a pod.' In Illustration 10, we see the interior of a London omnibus at this time and it does indeed look as though the passengers are crammed in like peas in a pod.

From time to time in recent years, people in Britain have objected that some traditional institution, famous shop or commercial enterprise has been taken over by a foreign company and there are murmurs of discontent to the effect that this would never have happened in the old days. This is nothing new. By 1855, there were literally hundreds of individual operators of buses in London. Many of these were single buses; owned and driven by one man. An estimated 20,000 people were being transported to work each day in London by buses. Matters were to reach a crisis, with a slump that year causing a rise in the price of horse feed. In Paris, the harsh economic climate ended with many smaller bus companies being taken over by larger concerns and ended in the unification of the French capital's buses under one company.

In London too, there were problems, with too many companies competing for trade. A French company founded that year, the Compagnie Generale des Omnibus de Londres, set out to rationalise the chaotic situation by buying out rivals and establishing a monopoly in London buses, just as had been done in Paris. Within a few years, they had done so and the 600 buses of the London General Omnibus Company, as it was now known, made it the biggest bus company in the world. Three-quarters of the buses in London were now owned and operated by a single company.

One bastion of independent buses were the De Tivoli patent omnibuses. These ran between Bayswater and London Bridge Station and were remarkable for the way in which they managed to emulate the three classes of railway transport. All the other buses in the middle of the nineteenth century were monopolised by middle-class users, although there were technically no first, second or third class tickets, as there were on the railways. This was simply by virtue of the cost of the tickets, which was prohibitively high for the average working man, although there was in theory no reason why labourers should not take the bus to work in the same way that commercial clerks did. There were those passengers, though, who felt that the London bus was too egalitarian and wished for something a little cheaper than a Hansom cab, but where they would not be expected to sit facing all sorts of strangers. The De Tivoli patent omnibus was the answer to their prayers. It was divided into three sections. At the front were two separate booths on either side, where first class passengers could sit, facing outward and entirely separate from other passengers. Then at the rear was a cabin with seating for four second class passengers. Third class was on the roof, a long bench running lengthways. The De Tivoli was not a notable success, largely because it could only carry half as many passengers as the buses of the Compagnie Generale des Omnibus de Londres.

The horse-drawn bus was an idea whose time had come. A year or two after it had made its appearance in London, the streets of provincial manufacturing cities such as Birmingham and Manchester were also full of buses. In Birmingham, there was a brief flirtation with steam buses, similar in many ways to the those which ran for a time in London. In 1832, two rival companies were running steam-powered buses between Birmingham and Bromsgrove. Neither of these companies were very successful and they could not compete with the horse buses which began running from 5 May 1834. The first regular bus services in Birmingham ran between Snow Hill and Edgbaston. Like those in London, they charged a fare of 6d, which effectively established them from the start as a middle-class means of transport. Other services soon followed, connecting Birmingham with the outlying districts of Handsworth, Smethwick and Small Heath. These buses were a great boon to commuters who had moved to the villages around Birmingham for reasons at which we looked in Chapter 1. In the northern city of Manchester, regular services by a horse-drawn coach began a little earlier, in 1824, although there is some debate as to whether this may properly be described as a bus. From 1830, horse buses were running between Manchester and Stockport, as well as from the Liverpool and Manchester Railway Terminus to Market Street.

These early bus services both served the needs of commuters and went a long way towards actually creating more commuters. Obviously, one of the disadvantages of living miles from one's place of work was that it entailed a wearisome journey by foot twice a day. It was this which had acted to discourage or at least limit the number of people moving house to live in the villages which lay a little way outside the big, industrial cities. Once a bus service was running though, it could not help but make those districts where it was running, more attractive to live in.

The role that the new forms of public transport played in the growth of commuting in the first few decades of Victoria's reign is therefore a complex one. New housing attracted entrepreneurs who might start a bus service in the area, but conversely, a new bus service might encourage builders to develop a district. Urban development was most noticeable along the lines of public transport routes, whether railways, buses or, in later years, trams. As the populations of British cities grew exponentially and they began to expand outwards into the surrounding countryside at this time, it is impossible to say whether the buses were stimulating the housing or if it was the other way round. All that we are able to say with assurance is that the cities were getting larger and that more or less at the same time, bus services were becoming more widespread.

The horse-drawn omnibus now ruled supreme as the middle-class commuter's favourite means of getting to the office; not only in London, but also in provincial cities as well. With the introduction of an upper deck, which came in the 1840s, a single London bus could carry twenty-five passengers at a time from the suburbs to the City and back again. From eight in the morning, the streets of the outer edges of British cities were crowded with buses taking clerks to their offices, shopkeepers to their premises and all manner of other white-collar workers to their places of work. Most working-class men still lived near enough to where they worked so that they could walk there. It would be another decade or so before commuting became a working-class way of life. When this happened, it would be not buses but trains to which they took and an unexpected consequence would be the widening of intellectual as well as spatial horizons.

Chapter 5

Expanding Cities and Opening Minds: The Working-Class Commuter

The commuters at whom we have so far looked belong almost invariably to the middle class. So ingrained is this association of commuting with the middle-class lifestyle, that the two things seem to go hand in hand, almost as a matter of course. Trying to re-imagine *Terry and June* as a comedy of working-class life conjures up a surreal vision of Alf Garnett in Surbiton or Purley. It simply wouldn't work!

This is very strange, because there have always been working-class commuters and they have, at some times and in various places, outnumbered those from the middle class. However, in the nineteenth century the two types tended to travel separately, often not even sharing the same type of transport. In Victorian Britain, buses, for instance, were almost exclusively the preserve of the middle-class commuter. Mr Pooter would not have had to sit next to a carpenter or plumber on his journey from Holloway to the City.

The history of working-class commuting has been rather neglected in British history, to such an extent that, as we saw above, the notion of a working-class commuter on television or in literature has a disconcerting air of unreality about it. It appears almost to be a contradiction in terms; we know very well that commuting is a white-collar lifestyle. This mindset is all the more peculiar when we examine the situation 150 years ago and reflect that not only was commuting very much a working-class way of life, but that it was actually of far greater importance to working-class men and women than it was to the commercial clerks who caught the bus to work each day. To middle-class workers, the daily commute was a tiresome necessity, the price they had to pay in order to live in a decent part of the city, with a house and garden of their own. For the working man, that same journey to work represented a liberation, an opportunity to change his very way of viewing the world and to develop a new sense of identity. It is perhaps no exaggeration to say that it was commuting which caused the urban proletariat of nineteenth-century Britain to become politically conscious and indirectly gave rise to the Labour Party. It is a sobering thought that it was commuting which perhaps ultimately produced politicians such as Clement Atlee and Tony Blair! This is, as we shall see, another of those aspects of commuting which had a very deep and abiding effect upon the whole country.

At the beginning of the nineteenth century, there was no reason for any working man or woman to live more than a short distance from their place of work. Even when the majority of the population had moved from an agrarian to an urban lifestyle, this remained the case. Those working in factories lived in cramped little houses and hovels within earshot of the factory whistle or bell which signalled the beginning of the working day. A recognised occupation of those days was the 'Knocker Upper', who went along a street rapping on the upper windows with a long stick or firing dried peas at bedroom windows with a peashooter, in order to alert the occupants to the fact that it was time to get up.

The growth of the working-class commuter had its roots, as is so often the case with national trends, in events in the capital. As those with the means to do so moved out into the newly built suburbs, the poorer people stayed huddled in the centre of London. Dickens' *Bleak House* describes vividly one of the so-called 'rookeries' to be found at this time in the heart of the greatest and most important city on earth. Tom-all-Alone is based upon many such places, districts like Seven Dials, near Covent Garden. In foetid cellars, crowded a dozen to a room, sleeping on floors, owning nothing other than the rags on their backs and living from hand to mouth, these were the wretched inhabitants of the city whose services respectable society needed, but did not wish otherwise to acknowledge. In Chapter 2, we looked at the production of bricks, an activity vital to the growth of the cities and without which, there would have been no cosy suburban villas for the likes of Mr Pooter and his family. However, brick makers were viewed, even by other working-class people, as being a particularly vicious and undesirable breed. These men and their families were an integral part of the building boom, but their living conditions were abominable. Often they were to be found in cheap lodging houses in the centre of London as they waited to hear of work.

This then was the situation in London in about 1840. Many working-class people were crammed into appalling accommodation in the middle of the city, while the middle classes decamped to the suburbs, where they were to become commuters. Then came the railways. In some European cities, the construction of railways was a carefully-planned enterprise, controlled by the state. This was not at all the case in Britain, where the doctrines of Malthus and Adam Smith held sway. It was a case of every man for himself and various companies began to be floated, whose only aim was to beat anybody else by building a railway linking the capital with provincial cities. There was a perfectly understandable tendency to avoid laying a railway line across the property of wealthy or influential men who might be disposed to fight this encroachment on their land through the courts. Delay could be fatal from a purely financial point of view and investors wanted quick returns, not complicated and costly lawsuits. For that reason, both the lines and the large stations needed to cope with the projected custom were established in areas where only poor, working class people lived. Few of these people owned their houses and most of them could therefore be turned out of their homes at a few days' notice.

The same thing happened when the Metropolitan Railway, the world's first underground railway, was built in London. The 'cut and cover' method of constructing the tunnels meant that many houses were demolished to make way for it. Incensed at the wholesale destruction of homes that he witnessed during the work on this and other railway lines in London, a vicar called William Denton published an attack on what he saw as the callousness of the capitalists and speculators who were causing such havoc to the lives of working class families in the capital. In *Observations on the Displacement of the Poor by Metropolitan Railways and Other Public Improvements*, Denton wrote that: 'The special lure of the capitalists is that the line will pass only through inferior property, that is through a densely peopled district, and will destroy the abode of the powerless and the poor, whilst it will avoid the properties of those whose opposition is to be dreaded – the great employers of labour.' Reverend Denton summed the matter up in a nutshell. For a brilliant picture of how the progress of a new railway line into London affected a poor district, we cannot do better than to turn once more to Dickens, who wrote in *Dombey and Son* of the railway making its way through Camden Town and the chaos which it created in quiet working-class streets:

> The first shock of a great earthquake had, just at that period, rent the whole neighbourhood to its centre. Traces of its course were visible on every side. Houses were knocked down; streets broken through and stopped; deep pits and trenches dug in the ground; enormous heaps of earth and clay thrown up; buildings that were undermined and shaking, propped by great beams of wood. Here, a chaos of carts, overthrown and jumbled together, lay topsy-turvy at the bottom of a steep, unnatural hill; there, confused treasures of iron soaked and rusted in something which had accidentally become a pond.

What a mercy that this hideous confusion and destruction should, as the Reverend Denton so shrewdly remarked, be taking place in, 'the abode of the powerless and poor', whose views and opinions on the subject could, it was hoped by those in charge of the enterprise, be safely ignored.

This slum clearance, for that was what it amounted to, was a disaster for poor people living in central London. Where compensation was offered, it typically amounted to a few shillings to encourage anybody who did have any sort of secure tenancy to surrender their rights. For most though, even two or three shillings was more than they could expect. These were the thousands of men and women who were paying a penny a night to share beds in a common lodging house. The house was sold to the railway company and swiftly demolished, leaving them to wander off in search of shelter elsewhere.

The sheer quantity of working-class housing destroyed as the railways forged their way into London is shocking to us today and, as the toll grew, even Parliament was compelled to take notice. The area around St Pancras, for example, had grown into a crowded slum after the construction of the canal which brought industry to that part of London. The subsequent building of the rail terminus meant driving thousands of people from their homes. When the North London Railway Company laid just two miles of track from Kingsland to Finsbury, they destroyed a thousand houses in the process. In Camden and Somers Town, 32,000 people were made homeless by the Midland Railway's new line.

There was no profit to be made by any businessman in providing alternative housing for those dispossessed by the activities of the railway companies. These were, after all, poor people. They would not be in the market for stucco-fronted villas in Holloway or Camberwell. The thousands of desperate people thrown out of their homes drifted off to swell other slums. No provision at all was made for them. Even if they could move to the suburbs, then their work would still be on the building sites and docks at the heart of the city. These were people who could not afford to waste a shilling a day on travelling by public transport.

The Victorian idea of a city was one where everybody conformed to certain standards of behaviour. The worst excesses of the Georgian Era, scenes such as those depicted in Hogarth's *Gin Lane*, did not at all accord with the vision of respectable city streets which was shaping the urban landscape at that time. As the scriptural text had it, the poor would always be with them, but that was no reason why they should be milling about the grand streets of the Metropolis without homes to go to! The obvious solution, both as a matter of *realpolitik* and also, one hopes, from a purely humanitarian perspective, was that something would have to be done about the overflowing slums of London and the growing number of people made homeless by the building of the railways.

The solution, when once Parliament addressed the problem, was obvious and just. It was the railway companies which had done much to create the problem, therefore the responsibility and cost for solving it should be laid upon their shoulders. The working classes were trapped near to their work because, unlike middle-class office workers, they could not afford to live in one place and work in another. Very well, the legislature would change the situation by passing a law which would enable ordinary working men to commute to work like their social superiors.

There were to be several Acts of Parliament aimed at reducing the slums of London by compelling railway companies to engage in what we would today perhaps call, 'social engineering'. One of the earliest was the Great Eastern Railways Act of 1864, which required that particular railway line to lay on workmen's trains, for which passengers would be charged just a penny for the entire journey. At a time when a penny a mile was the average cost of an urban railway journey, this represented an enormous saving for men and women for whom every penny was precious. The Act specified which stations would have to offer these greatly reduced fares; they included Walthamstow and Edmonton, to the north of the capital. One train a day was to depart for town before seven in the morning and another to return after six in the evening. It will be recalled that one of the reasons that buses were not really used by working men to commute was that they didn't start running until eight in the morning, by which time most of them would already have been expected to be at work.

The Acts of Parliament which made workmen's fares a legal requirement, effectively introduced a fourth class of travel on the railways, the so-called 'Parliamentary' train. When railways first began running in this country, it seemed logical to make provision for three classes of passenger. Upper-class people would naturally travel first class, the middle classes would use second class and the working classes would go by third. Tickets for workmen's trains were classified as 'Parliamentary third class'. Actually, second class travel fell into disuse in the 1870s, leaving a strange situation, which lingered on for almost a century, whereby only first and third class travel was provided. The reason for this was that the offer of third class travel was actually a legal requirement for railway companies, under the Railway Regulation Act of 1844. Even after the end of the Second World War, British Railways offered first or third class tickets, but no second. In 1956, this strange anomaly was rectified and third class tickets were reclassified as second class. Passengers from a workmen's train may be seen in Illustration 11.

Like many of the companies which were required by law to run cheap trains in this way, the Great Eastern actually began to exceed their legal duty and by the turn of the century were operating ten workmen's trains a day, running to stations as far as eleven miles from the centre of London. The large number of passengers being carried, and the eventual abolition of passenger duty on those charging less than 1d (½p) a mile for journeys, made the running of such trains profitable, despite the vastly reduced fares being charge.

From 1864 onwards, every time Parliament passed an Act allowing for the opening or expansion of a railway line, a clause was inserted which obliged the company, as a condition of being given permission to set up the line, to run cheap trains for working-class commuters. The Cheap Trains Act of 1883 simplified the various legislation, giving a general financial inducement to the railways to reduce their fares and enable working people to live in suburbs and commute to work each day, not only in London but across the whole country. Passenger duty was abolished for any train charging less than 1d a mile and the act also enforced the general principle of cheap trains to be run every day.

Even before the 1883 Act laid these legal obligations generally upon railway companies, many had got into the habit of offering cheaper fares early in the morning and later in the evening; specifically to encourage working men and women to use their trains. In the year before the passing of the Cheap Trains Act, 25,671 workmen's tickets were being issued every day in London and its surrounding suburbs.

As late as 1873, a magazine written for and about working men had observed that large numbers of working-class people never travelled by train. The various Acts relating to workmen's trains, together with the independent actions of the railways themselves, brought about a dramatic change in this respect. Working-class commuters began to outnumber those from the middle classes. At the same time, there was now an impetus to develop specifically working-class suburbs for skilled manual workers and artisans. This trend forced white-collar workers to move even further out towards newer suburbs. Successive waves of commuters thus colonised suburbs and were in turn displaced by those of lower social standing as the years went by. Larger houses in suburbs which were becoming working class were split into smaller flats and new terraces of smaller houses. The Cheap Trains Act first precipitated and then greatly accelerated this process.

These outward waves of population, based upon class, have in recent years been replaced by similar shifts in population based not upon class, but race. In the nineteenth century, upper middle-class people would first move into a district on the very edge of a city. There, they would have houses built for themselves and so a new suburb would at first consist of large detached villas, each surrounded by an acre or two of garden. These people would be successful businessmen, factory owners and others with plenty of money. Sooner or later, property speculators and builders would take an interest in such an area and buy up nearby farmland, which would soon become a heaving riot of brick fields and building sites, as new streets were laid out and built. These new houses would be terraces of modest properties which would be rented to clerks and shop assistants. What was once a smart and wealthy suburb would thus become less desirable and those with the means to do so would move even further out, in a bid to escape the rows of suburban houses which were now threatening to choke off their pleasant, semi-rural idyll. As these waves of slightly different social groups passed through an area, the general and overall trend would be for it to sink in desirability for those who were aware of such social niceties. After Mr Pooter's son Lupin had stayed for a while at his father's house, he decided to take a furnished apartment in Bayswater, on the grounds that Brickfield Terrace was a bit 'off'. By this, he meant that only lower middle-class people like his father lived in that part of Holloway. Eventually, such suburbs would sink even further and become working-class areas. Ultimately, houses would be split up into several rented flats and when that happened, a neighbourhood really had reached the bottom rung of respectability!

A by-product both of the trends outlined above, together with the provision of cheap fares to encourage workmen to use the railways to travel to work, was the creation of the first working-class suburbs in north and east London. Speculative builders saw that here was a market for which it might be worth catering; respectable, hardworking men able to afford the rent of a house or who might even be in a position in the future actually to buy a property. Police officers, firemen, foremen in factories and other in the same class began to live the commuter lifestyle.

The reason that it was now profitable to cater for the needs of working class families by building houses specifically for them, was that the standard of living for people in the lower socio-economic categories was rising faster than it had ever done before. The urban proletariat of Britain not only had money now to pay for the rent of decent houses, many of them even had a surplus, when all the necessities of life had been paid for, to spend on leisure. This rise in disposable income among working class people coincided, happily, with the provision of cheap transport such as workmen's trains and trams. Two particular periods of rising prosperity were 1868 to 1874 and 1880 to 1896. During the second of those periods, real wages rose by nearly 46 per cent. This was in direct contravention of the so-called 'Iron Law of Wages' proposed by Karl Marx, which held that real wages always tend towards the bare minimum necessary to sustain the life of the worker.

Another factor was also at work which had the effect of increasing the prosperity of working-class families. For reasons which are still unclear, the trend was for married couples to have fewer children. This naturally meant that they had more money available to them. It will be recalled that when Charles Dickens wrote of the lower middle-class clerks hurrying to work in the City from walking suburbs such as Camden, he talked of 'middle-aged men, whose salaries have by no means increased in the same proportion as their families'. In other words, they were having more and more children which they could ill afford and this led them, like Bob Cratchit, into poverty. Now, things were changing. Salaries were increasing in a greater proportion than the size of their families. With smaller families and higher wages, there was ample money available in many families for improved housing.

Obviously, while the working class had insufficient money to pay for the rent of new houses, it would have been quixotic of any builder to embark upon such projects as the construction of whole streets designed specifically for this class. Now though, people like that could not only afford to rent, some would even be obtaining mortgages or find that they could save enough to buy a house outright. The working-class commuter boom had begun.

The new working-class suburbs in London grew at an astonishing pace and were, naturally enough, centred around railway stations. Walthamstow, West Ham, Tottenham and Willesden; these districts all doubled in size and population in the space of a decade or so. In fact these new working-class commuter districts were growing faster than anywhere else in the entire country. West Ham, for example, had just 19,000 residents in 1851. Forty years later, 267,000 people were living there. Willesden, another of these suburbs, provides us with a perfect example of how a different class of commuter tended to drive out those higher on the social scale. Until the 1870s, Willesden had been almost a rural area, with only a handful of large detached villas belonging to bankers and financiers. As the builders moved in and refashioned Willesden into a working-class area, the well-to-do decamped, heading further out to places like Ealing and Hendon.

A century or so later, these areas which had moved down the Victorian social scale, from being the home of wealthy bankers to becoming first middle-class and then working-class suburbs, underwent yet another transformation, when the white working class inhabitants in their turn moved further out from the centre of London; giving way to various groups of Commonwealth immigrants. Tottenham and Willesden are today primarily black areas, while Walthamstow and West Ham have a very high proportion of families from south Asia. This changing composition merely continues an old tradition.

At the beginning of this chapter, it was suggested that the adoption by working-class people of the commuting lifestyle caused great political changes and was indirectly responsible for bringing into existence one of the main political forces in Britain; the Labour Party. It is possible that some readers might have taken this to be mere hyperbole, but that is far from being the case. To understand the significance of the transformation of many working-class men and women into commuters, it will be necessary to consider one or two other aspects of the railways which were beginning to reach all parts of the country at that time. Before we do so though, it might be helpful to look at the views of one of the workmen travelling home from his labour at the end of the day in 1865. Henry Mayhew, the indefatigable chronicler of Victorian London, wrote in *Shops and Companies of London* of the views that working men had given him about the advantages of the newly opened Metropolitan Railway train in which they were travelling. One man said that without the railway, which he was now able to use because of the cheap fares, he would have had to walk six miles to and from work each day. Another passenger expanded on the advantages of commuting for men such as them, saying 'Just think of what these here trains save you at night after your work's over. If a man gets home tired after his day's labour he is inclined to be quarrelsome with his missus and the children, and this leads to all kinds of noises, and ends in him going off to the pub for a little bit of quiet: while if he gets a ride home, and has a good rest after he has knocked off for the day, I can tell you he is as pleasant a fellow again over his supper.' In other words, affordable public transport was making the home lives of many working men more agreeable and causing them to be less apt to make a beeline for the public house as soon as they finished work. This was an interesting perspective, but there was a lot more to the newly-acquired habit of commuting among working men than just not rowing with the wife and ending up at the pub! To understand the fuller implications, we need to look at what was to become a major social and intellectual event in British life: ready access to affordable books.

In 1792, a man called Henry Walton Smith set up as a news vendor in London. In time, Henry Walton Smith's sons, Henry Edward and William Henry took over the business. William Henry Smith proved to be the better businessman of the two and so he assumed control of the firm, bringing his son into partnership with him. As a result, from 1846 onwards, the firm became known as W. H. Smith and Son. Two years later, perhaps under the influence of a dynamic young man in his early twenties, W. H. Smith opened their first news stand at a railway station. The venture, at Euston, was an instant success. The railway boom was in full swing and passengers were glad to be able to buy newspapers, magazines and books to while away the time as they waited for their train to arrive, or to read when the train was rattling through the countryside. Reading while actually travelling was a novelty: the swaying and bumping of stagecoaches had previously made such an activity all but impossible on journeys from city to city.

LEAVE THIS
AND

"I never had any other desire so strong and so like to covetousness as that one which I have had always, that I might be Master of a small House and a Large Garden, with moderate conveniences joined to them."

Abraham Cowley

MOVE TO EDGWARE

1. An invitation to Metro-land, a commuter's paradise.

2. The roots of the British commuting lifestyle lie buried 250 million years in the past.

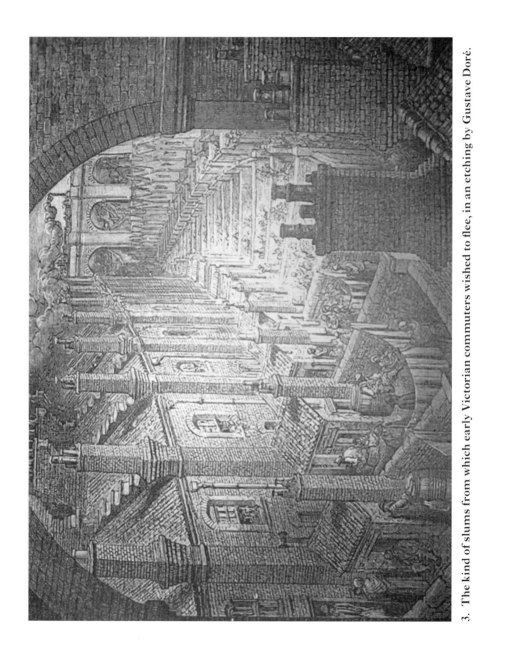

3. The kind of slums from which early Victorian commuters wished to flee, in an etching by Gustave Doré.

4. The first fictional commuter, Bob Cratchit of Dicken's *A Christmas Carol*.

5. London Bridge to Greenwich, the world's first commuter railway.

6. One of the last brick kilns remaining in London, to be found in Holland Park.

LONDON going out of Town — or —— The March of Bricks & Mortar!

Designed Etched & Published by George Cruickshank — November 1st 1829 —

7. *London going Out of Town — or The March of Bricks and Mortar*, by George Cruickshank, published in 1829.

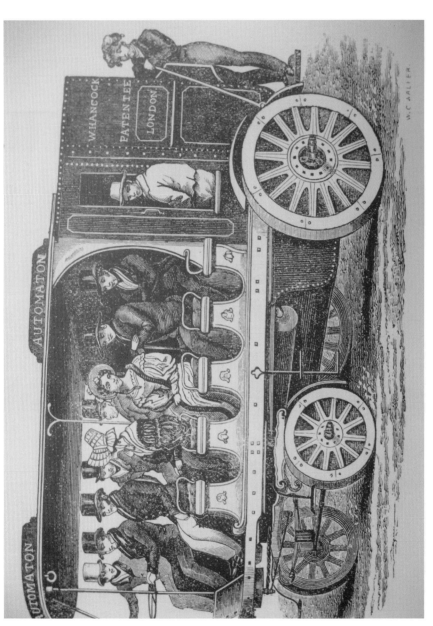

8. Walter Hancock's *Automaton* in 1839, one of the first steam-driven buses in London.

9. **Mr Pooter, hero of** *The Diary of a Nobody*, **adds style to his home by putting up a plaster-of-paris stag's head.**

10. The crowded interior of an early omnibus.

11. Working-class commuters arriving on an early-morning 'Parliamentary' workmen's train.

12. The last surviving fragment of London's once-extensive tramlines, in Southampton Row.

HANSOM CAB photographed in London in 1895. (Smithsonian photo.)

13. The Hansom cab, another popular means of transport for the wealthier commuter.

14. The dummy houses in London's Leinster Gardens that conceal the railway line.

15. Britain's first electric tram, at Northfleet in Kent in 1889.

16. The Aldersgate bombing of 1897, the first fatal terrorist attack on the London Underground.

17. A commuter's life in Golders Green, in a mock-Tudor semi, as shown in a poster advertising the delights of Metro-land.

18. The dream of many commuters: a typical mock-Tudor semi from the 1930s.

19. More examples of fine mock-Tudor properties for commuters.

20. Strap-hangers on the Tube in the rush hour.

We are now so used to cheap books being universally available wherever we might be, that it might be necessary to pause at this point and consider just how revolutionary W. H. Smith's venture actually was. At the time that the first W. H. Smith's stand was opened at Euston, the typical novel consisted of three volumes and when published cost about thirty shillings or £1.50. We might remember that Bob Cratchit was at that time earning only fifteen shillings (75p) a week. In other words, buying a new novel would have cost two weeks' wages for an ordinary clerk. In effect, books were luxury items, beyond the reach of all but the wealthy. If a City clerk could not afford to buy the latest novel; what hope for working-class men and women? All this was to change in the course of only a few years and it was the railways and W. H. Smith which were largely responsible for this important development.

In the same year that the first W. H. Smith's newsstand in a station was opened, the publisher Routledge began production of what they called their 'Railway Library'. These were cheap books, reprints of novels which had already been published in expensive editions. It was only natural for W. H. Smith to begin stocking these books and they were an immediate and huge success. For the first time in British history, the ownership of books was possible for anybody with a relatively modest sum of money at his or her disposal. A whole new genre of 'Railway fiction' had been born. As it became more and more popular, an awful lot of stupendously trashy detective novels and romances were churned out; the pulp fiction of Victorian Britain. With regular railway travel now becoming a feature of working-class life, for reasons at which we looked above, those using the cheap workmen's trains too began to buy the books on sale at railway stations. Within a few years, absolutely everybody travelling by train was reading either a newspaper or book. This was so revolutionary that contemporary commentators remarked on the phenomenon with something approaching awe. Long before the end of the century, every working man and woman was reading avidly during the journey to work. One observer wrote in 1893: 'The clerks and artisans, shopgirls, dressmakers, and milliners, who pour into London every morning by the early trains, have, each and every one, a choice specimen of penny fiction with which to beguile the short journey, and perhaps the few spare minutes of a busy day. The workingman who slouches up and down the platform, waiting for the moment of departure, is absorbed in some crumpled bit of pink-covered romance.' In addition to what is rather snobbishly described as 'penny fiction', many far more worthy works of literature were being bought and read by working men and women on the train to work in the morning. The cheapest editions were of books whose copyright had expired. These books were especially popular with working-class commuters, because they were so reasonably priced. As a consequence, the most popular authors among many of the manual workers who were now commuting into Central London each morning were not the writers of detective fiction, but men like Daniel Defoe, Oliver Goldsmith and Henry Fielding. The sight of a labourer reading *The Vicar of Wakefield* or *Robinson Crusoe* was a common one on the early-morning trains into the City, from the 1850s onwards. Once again, Dickens noted this phenomenon and duly incorporated it into one of his own novels, in this case *Hard Times*. Talking of the reading habits of the factory workers in the fictional Coketown, Dickens writes: 'They wondered about human nature, human passions, human hopes and fears, the struggles, triumphs and defeats, the cares and joys and sorrows, the lives and deaths of common men and women! They sometimes, after fifteen hour's work, sat down to read mere fables about men and women more or less like themselves, and about children, more or less like their own. They took De Foe to their bosoms, instead of Euclid, and seemed to be on the whole more comforted by Goldsmith than by Cocker.' Both in London and other industrial cities, the workers in factories, labourers in markets, dockers, policemen and bus drivers were regularly reading great classics of English literature, not because they were hoping to gain GCSEs or A Levels in the subject, but purely for their own pleasure. Thanks to the new custom of commuting, they now had an hour or so each day for the uninterrupted reading of such novels.

Nor was it only novels that were being eagerly read by working-class commuters. There was a great market for books about self-improvement as well. William Henry Smith was very particular about the sort of books stocked in his outlets at railways stations; the satirical magazine *Punch* used to call him 'Old Morality'. His bookstalls would never display anything which might offend the most delicate sensibilities. Being the product of a self-made man, he was keen to extol the virtues of striving to better oneself and sold, alongside the novels, such Victorian classics as Samuel Smiles' *Self-Help; with Illustrations of Character and Conduct*. This book, and many others of the same type, encouraged working men to better themselves, avoiding drinking in favour of study. In this way, it was claimed, they would be able to raise themselves up the social scale and be free of the threat of poverty.

Throughout much of British history, it was considered a virtue to be content in one's station in life. Ambition was thought to be associated with the sin of pride; the kind of thing which led Lucifer to rebel against God. Working people were taught by the church that acceptance of their lowly state was a religious virtue and that it was wrong to try and rise higher than they had been born. We hear an echo of these sentiments in that most beloved of Victorian hymns, *All Things Bright and Beautiful*:

The rich man in his castle,
The poor man at his gate,
God made them high or lowly,
And ordered their estate.

Now, these 'lowly' people had been given both the leisure to read for an hour or so each day and also provided with affordable material, not only in the form of literary classics, but also books exhorting them to work at changing their situation in life. Ambition was now being presented to working-class people as not sinful, but rather a wise and desirable state of mind. Writing in 1865, Andrew Wynter described the popularity at railway stations of books of this kind: 'Perhaps the most cheering feature in the demand for cheap editions of books, is the call for works of the character of "Self-Help" and "Stephenson's Life". The success of these works has called forth a host of Imitations, called, "Men Who have Risen", "Men in Earnest", "Men Who have Made Themselves", "Farmer's Boys" and others, all testifying to the love of energetic action among the population so different to that which obtains in centralized continental countries.'

The books being sold by W. H. Smith's outlets at stations were cheap, but they were still too expensive for some. In 1860, the company opened their first lending library, where books could be borrowed for a penny a day. This was arranged in such a way that one could borrow a book from one branch and then return it to another. These libraries contained non-fiction as well as novels and soon became very popular with working-class commuters. They were now able to study politics, history and law on their way to work, if they were so minded. There were public libraries in Britain from 1850 onwards, but they were, at first, few and far between and some did not encourage working-class members. It was W. H. Smith and the new habit of commuting which brought ordinary working men into contact with all sorts of new ideas about society, religion and many other subjects. Having their mental horizons broadened in this way led to workers becoming dissatisfied with the existing social system and they were now able to compare their situation not only with those of people in the past, but also to imagine possible future political arrangements which would be very different from those then prevailing. Charles Darwin's *On the Origin of Species* was stocked, as was *Capital* by Karl Marx. So popular was the W. H. Smith lending library that it lingered on for a little over a century, the last branch closing in 1961. Together, W. H. Smith and the cheap commuter trains transformed the intellectual lives of many working-class people living in and around British cities. It is not unreasonable to suggest that these two factors were responsible for the rise in political consciousness among working people which led at the end of the nineteenth century to the establishment of the Labour Party.

If buses were predominantly a middle-class way of transporting commuters into cities and trains were shared, albeit used generally at different times, there was one means of public transport used by commuters which was almost exclusively working class. In an earlier chapter, it was remarked that a geological map of Britain showing accessible deposits of coal would be very similar to an epidemiological one illustrating infant mortality rates. This is of course because there was a direct correlation between the industrialisation of certain areas and the poor lifestyle of those who then went to work in the factories, mines and foundries of the newly-developing areas. Precisely the same distribution would have been seen on a map of Britain if we were to look for towns which had more than ten miles of municipal tramways by 1899; Glasgow, Edinburgh, Newcastle, Liverpool, Bradford, Sheffield, Stoke-on-Trent, Birmingham, Walsall, Dudley and London.

The world's first tram for passengers was the Swansea and Mumbles Railway in Wales, which opened in 1804. It had at first been intended only for industrial use, but from 1807 onwards was soon carrying passengers as well. This horse-drawn tram proved very popular with people living in the area; there being no road link at that time between Swansea and Oystermouth. The tram as we know it though was an essentially urban vehicle and the first British city in which they began running was London.

The rationale behind the introduction of trams was simple; they could carry more passengers than buses and would therefore be cheaper to run and could charge lower fares. Both the operators and passengers would consequently benefit. There was a false start in the setting up of trams on the streets of Britain's cities, when an American businessman with the marvellously apposite name of George Train set up a tramway in Victoria Street in Westminster. Train believed that he had obtained permission for this, but the police and local authorities disagreed and he was arrested and prosecuted for 'breaking and injuring' the street. The problem was that the rails on which his trams were travelling were just like ordinary railway lines and proved a great inconvenience to other vehicles using the road. After the failure of his London tramway, George Train went north and set up the Darlington Street Railway Company, which also failed after a few years.

A few words about the mechanics of running trams might be useful at this point. A lot of the effort involved in moving a bus from place to place was overcoming the friction between the wheels of the vehicle and the surface of the road. Persuading the wheels to grind their way through mud, dirt and refuse or along a road which had no properly-constructed surface, took up a lot of energy. A tram's metal wheels, rolling along metal rails, meant a huge reduction in friction and so a greater load could be transported by use of the same power. A tram might be able to carry fifty passengers, twice as many as a bus. This would make them, of course, cheaper to run. The rails upon which the carriage moved did not necessarily have to be raised proud of the roadway, which was where George Train's early attempts at what he called 'Street Railways' got into difficulties. Rails could be recessed, a little below the surface of the road, which meant that other vehicles would not be obstructed and pedestrians would be less apt to trip over them. Two further advantages of trams over buses were that they ran far more smoothly and comfortably and were safer, with less risk of collisions.

During the 1860s, plans were made for setting up tram services in London and other cities. A demonstration tramway was opened at Crystal Palace and in 1870 Parliament passed the Tramways Act. This authorised local authorities to grant 21-year leases to private operators and allow them to install tram tracks along public roads. At the end of that period, the councils could take over and run the trams themselves, if they wished, by buying out the companies who had been running them. Fares were to be set at 1d (½p) a mile, with half price workmen's fares for early and late journeys. The fact that trams would be running early in the morning made them, regardless of the cheaper fares, attractive to working-class men and women. Those living in suburbs such as Camberwell, Stratford and Peckham would now have an even cheaper means of getting into the centre of London than the early morning trains. At ½d a journey, the tram was half the price of a workmen's train.

Where London led, other cities followed. The first trams in Edinburgh began running on 6 November 1871, when the Edinburgh Street Tramways Company's tramway between Haymarket and Bernard Street went into operation. In August 1872, the Glasgow Tramway and Omnibus Company opened the St George's to Eglinton tramline and this was soon extended. Other cities followed, including Manchester which, from 1877, had the Manchester Suburban Tramways Company operating trams to and from the suburbs.

It was tacitly understood from the beginning that trams were a working-class means of transport. This accounted for the fact that in London trams were never allowed to run through either the City of London itself or the West End. It was felt that the sight of trams clanging through the streets of a city's commercial centre might be all very well in Scotland or the north of England, but would not really be quite the thing for Oxford Street or Threadneedle Street! The closest that any trams came to London's West End was in 1908, when a tunnel was built to connect the tramway of south London with those of the northern part of the city. This ran from Theobald's Road, diving under Kingsway and not emerging until it was at Waterloo Bridge.

As the network of trams in London extended and as other cities allowed companies to set up and operate trams, the suburbs began to change. Cheap railway fares had begun the process, but it was greatly accelerated by the trams: the inner suburbs were no longer the only ones colonised by the working classes. As tramlines snaked out further and further from city centres, so speculative builders moved in and created new districts. Since it was in general working class people who used the trams; these were from the beginning working-class suburbs. This expansion of predominantly industrial cities along the axes of the new tramlines gave many cities a configuration somewhat reminiscent of starfish with long, thin points radiating out into the countryside.

It was in the Midlands and north of England that trams became the universal means of transport for many ordinary people. The city-wide networks extended so far that they almost, and in some cases actually did, touch the networks in neighbouring cities. This meant that trams could be used by working men as not just a local method of transport, but for long-distance journeys as well. The classic example of this tendency of neighbouring tramlines to reach adjacent areas was provided by the north of England, where it was possible to travel from Leeds to Liverpool by tram, with only short walks at either end of various systems. In this way, one could ride from the centre of Leeds to the outskirts of the city, where the Leeds trams almost connected with those of Bradford and Huddersfield. Then it was only another short walk to the outlying lines of the Manchester trams and then via Warrington to Liverpool.

Just as suburban trains and the London Underground gave working-class people the chance to read as they travelled to and from their places of work; so too with trams. The sight of a tram full of working men with their noses buried in newspapers and books became common in the industrial heartlands of northern Britain. As the nineteenth century drew on, the public transport which carried working-class commuters acted increasingly as a way of widening their horizons not only in the purely physical sense of enabling them to travel cheaply further and further afield, but also by giving them time and leisure to broaden their intellectual horizons by reading affordable editions of books. The benefits of trams for the working-class populations of the burgeoning cities of Britain was not limited to their physical and intellectual liberation. They also exerted a powerful influence upon their way of life of them and that of their children in another way.

In Chapter 1, we saw that the living conditions of the urban proletariat in the early part of the nineteenth century were unbelievably grim. If the buses and trains first let the middle classes move out into more spacious and sanitary accommodation, then the trams performed a similar service for the working class. From the 1870s onwards, more and more working people were able to escape from the crowded and unhealthy housing in which they had been trapped since the beginning of the Industrial Revolution. This process, which began with the cheap workmen's tickets on the suburban railways of London, accelerated greatly with the building of more and more tramlines.

Although aiding working-class people to adopt the commuting way of life and to encourage them to move out of city centre slums was the primary motive for the establishment of trams, particularly when they were later electrified, there was a side effect, which also proved beneficial to working families. Richard Hoggart, the Leeds born academic, famously described trams as 'the gondolas of the people'. he meant by this that trams were more than merely a means by which working men and women were transported to the factories and mills in which they worked. They also took them to football matches, picnics and trips to the seaside. Apart from the cheap workmen's tickets, railway travel was always a little too expensive for the average working man to use on a regular basis. The trams, on the other hand, cost only a penny or two to travel in for miles. Illustration 12 shows the last remaining fragment in London of this most popular means of transport. A stretch of cobbled roadway, with the tramlines set into it, somehow survives in Southampton Row in central London.

In London, by the end of the nineteenth century a family living in the slums of Bethnal Green could travel by tram to Epping Forest and Hampstead, or even out into the countryside around Ponders End. Those in Leeds could take a succession of trams at a penny a time and end up on the west coast. The tram certainly liberated working-class families in a physical sense, but it opened up horizons mentally as well. Before the advent of trams, a child might spend the first ten or fifteen years of his life, never venturing more than a mile or two from the house where he had been born. In the mid-nineteenth century, the outlooks and lives of many children in the slums of Britain's great industrial cities were as restricted as circumscribed as those of a peasant living in a medieval village. The fantastically cheap travel provided by the new networks of tramlines put an end to that. From then on, children and young people were able to compare their own environment with that of others living in and around the city in which they had grown up. They consequently became aware that theirs was not the only way of life and that others were richer and sometimes poorer than they themselves. They learned that not everybody lived in crowded tenements and cramped back-to-backs near factories and workshops. This too, like the ready availability of cheap books, acted as a spur to ambition.

We have followed the growth of the custom of commuting to work from the beginning of the Industrial Revolution until the end of the nineteenth century, which was coincidentally about the same time that the Victorian Era came to an end. We have seen that the introduction of public transport of which all classes and conditions of men and women could take advantage, had the effect of both causing the cities of Britain to grow outwards, while at the same time allowing the minds of those using the buses, trains and trams to be nourished and nurtured through the medium of printed material and also by seeing other parts of the country, beyond the districts in which they themselves lived. This may sound to us today a trifling matter, but to people who had never before owned a book or moved more than a couple of miles from their homes and workplaces, it was anything but.

Before looking at how commuting developed in the twentieth century, we shall look at the psychology of this way of life. The practice of commuting brought about various changes which affected not only those who were actually undertaking the journey to work each day on public transport, but also had a wider impact upon the whole nation.

Chapter 6

Exploring the Liminal Zone: The Psychology of Commuting

Any exploration of the psychology of commuting must surely begin with that greatest of fetishes for the dedicated commuter; punctuality. We have already observed that precise timekeeping is an integral part of the commuter's daily routine. It would be no good going off to Town on the 8:21 every morning, like Mr Brown in the theme song of *Dad's Army,* if you were not conscious to the very minute of what the time was, while you ate breakfast and cleaned your teeth. From the writings of Dickens and Jerome K. Jerome through to the adventures of Reginald Perrin, the commuter's obsessive interest in the correct time has been recognised as a defining characteristic of the lifestyle. To understand how and why this preoccupation with time arose, it is necessary to look back into the past and see how time was viewed before there were commuters to fret about getting to the office on time.

Before the Industrial Revolution, time was governed less by clocks and watches than by the rising and setting of the sun. Work in the fields began at dawn and when the sun was at its zenith; that was a convenient time to stop working and eat. The setting of the sun was a reasonable time to end work. Of course, the sun rises earlier and sets later in the summer than it does in the winter, but that too suits an agrarian way of life. There is always more to do on a farm in the summer than there is in December and so it makes sense to begin work earlier at that time of year. The seasons too were an important part of the rhythm of time before there were factories and steam engines.

Until the Industrial Revolution, it was of no conceivable relevance to the average worker that the day was divided into twenty-four hours, still less that each of those hours was further subdivided into sixty minutes. The church bell would tell them when it was time to pray or to attend divine worship, the sun informed them when they should rise from their beds. That anybody would be concerned with a period of time as short as a minute was quite beyond the comprehension of any agricultural worker. In a field of wheat, nothing much happens in the space of sixty seconds! It was altogether possible to grow up in a farming community and reach adulthood without being aware of the arbitrary division of time into hours and minutes. Telling the time was a skill of little or no practical use.

Local time varied in Britain prior to the nineteenth century. It was calculated according to longitude, meaning that Bristol was ten minutes behind London. Once railways were built and timetables written, it then became essential for the whole country to run to the same time. That time had also to be precise to the minute or even, ideally, to the very second. It might not matter much if the harvesting of wheat began fifteen minutes before or after dawn, but it certainly made a good deal of difference if two trains were going to be running along the same track at intervals of a quarter of an hour! This need for absolutely accurate timekeeping was demonstrated in the United States on 18 April 1891, when the pocket watch of an engineer on one train stopped for four minutes and then started again. Not realising that this had happened led to disaster; as another train was due to reach a set of points in Kipton, Ohio, four minutes after the first train. As it was; the two trains arrived simultaneously and collided, with tragic results. Nine men were killed. Just four minutes had made the difference between life and death. A consequence of this terrible accident was the accelerated development of cheap, mass-produced pocket watches. It was these which brought accurate time-keeping within reach of the masses.

Incidents like the Kipton train crash demonstrated the vital need for accurate timekeeping when running railways. Whether news of such disasters was absorbed subliminally by Victorian commuters, it is impossible to say. What is absolutely certain is that by the end of the century, the commuter running for a train was such a common figure that when Jerome K. Jerome described Uncle Podger racing to catch his train in the morning at Ealing, the image was instantly recognisable to the reading public.

To be a commuter by public transport meant, and means still, being bound by the clock more than other workers. If I walk to work and find that I am a little late, I can walk faster or even run if need be. Travelling by public transport though, alters the case dramatically. If I miss that vital bus or train to the city, then there is nothing for it but to stand and wait for the next one. I am no longer master of my own time, but am compelled to wait upon the pleasure of others. A minute either way under such circumstances can mean the difference between being a few minutes early for work and being half an hour late. This will all sound absurdly obvious to a seasoned commuter today, but at first, during the mid-nineteenth century, took a lot of getting used to.

This precise awareness of time began with the operation of factories and railways in Britain, but at first, travel in this way was far from being a regular event for many people. When one only travels by train once or twice a year, then it is an important event and one will tend naturally to get to the station well ahead of time; it is, after all, a special occasion. If, on the other hand, you are going to be catching trains or buses twice a day, for six days a week, you will wish to cut down to an absolute bare minimum the amount of time that you spend hanging around waiting for the bus or train. This requires an accurate knowledge of the time; precise to within a minute or two.

So much for punctuality. It is time now to consider another aspect of commuting which any commuter will probably take for granted, without ever having thought about the matter over-much. One of the first things that a visitor from abroad learns when travelling on the London Underground is that there is a very powerful and ingrained tradition of utterly ignoring one's fellow passengers. This fixed determination to ignore anybody else in the carriage, no matter how strange their appearance or eccentric their behaviour, began with nineteenth-century commuters and has been honed over a century and a half into a precise art. Travelling to work on public transport is an intensely private and personal experience. Whatever John Donne might have said on the subject of no man being an island may be completely disregarded on the train journey to work. An island is precisely what every man and woman is, at least on the 8:14 to Victoria. Even making fleeting eye contact with those in the same carriage is a grave breach of etiquette. No matter that one might be forced to stand with one's face six inches in front of a complete stranger while you both try and maintain balance as the Tube train sways back and forth; you do not under any circumstances acknowledge that other person's existence.

The reasons behind this strange, almost autistic aversion to human contact during the journey to work have their roots in the past. Using public transport was once an exceptional and rare event, something which might be undertaken once every few years, by those with a fair amount of money to spend. Hardly anybody travelled regularly by stagecoach and so the very novelty tended to break the ice and allow strangers to talk freely to each other. This informality was maintained to a certain extent during the operation of the first railway trains. Passengers were divided up into first, second and third class and so one might be reasonably sure of at least sharing a carriage with those of a similar social standing to oneself. More importantly, these were people whom one would never encounter again. Chatting to a stranger during an extraordinary event was permissible; even in Britain of the 1830s.

One has to bear in mind the strict rules which regulated social intercourse, particularly among the middle classes. It was not in general permitted even to talk to a person unless one had been properly introduced. Fortunately, society was so regulated that the chances were that one would not find oneself sitting opposite anybody without first being introduced. The railway train overthrew all these conventions.

Books on etiquette dealt neatly with the problem of how to get by on trains, by decreeing that it was acceptable to converse with strangers if you found yourself sharing a carriage, but that after the journey was over, you should then ignore the travelling companion even if you met him or her in the street. Ordinary conventions were suspended during the length of a journey, but immediately resumed once you both left the train.

Once the experience of going from place to place by train was no longer an exciting novelty, the natural British reserve began to creep back. When a way of life began in which one might find oneself facing the same strangers not merely during the odd journey, but every single day, then something needed to give. Passengers fell back into the ordinary rules of introductions and other social intercourse. This meant of course that unless one had been properly introduced to somebody, one could hardly even acknowledge him. This promised to lead to great embarrassment, as people might inadvertently make eye contact and feel impelled to begin a conversation.

One of the neatest ways of avoiding being drawn into the company of others without simply staring at them and refusing to engage in conversation is of course by engrossing yourself in a newspaper, magazine or book. When George Shillibeer launched his omnibuses in 1829, they were provided with plenty of reading material, perhaps for this reason. Thus, from the very beginning of the practice of commuting by public transport, passengers were able to prevent awkwardness by keeping their eyes fixed firmly on a line of print, instead of inadvertently catching the eye of a fellow traveller.

For more than 150 years, this was very much the custom for commuters on buses, trams, trains and the Underground. Observers of Victorian London remarked that every single person on Tube trains and trams was sure to be reading and this continued right up until the last decade or so. The traditional image of the commuter carrying a copy of *The Times* indicates that the real commuter always had some reading material with him. The newspapers acted as shields, behind which commuters were able to retreat to avoid the company of others. Over the last few years, there has been a change and instead of reading newspapers and books, almost every commuter now has either a mobile telephone, e-reader or tablet to stare at. The rare travellers who lack such things almost invariably manage to isolate themselves by having earphones.

To understand fully the phenomenon of commuting, it is necessary to consider two distinct and antagonistic aspects of the process. The first of these is the fixed or ritual nature of the journeys which are undertaken each day; the second that commuting itself is, on the contrary, about transformation and change. The fine balancing of these opposing forces of change and stability is an integral part of commuting.

The first point to be grasped is that commuting is an in-between stage. Most of us have different personas according to where we are and whom we are meeting. We tend to talk and behave in a completely dissimilar way at work than we do at home with our family. The way we comport ourselves when visiting our parents will typically differ radically from our conduct on a night out with our mates. It is a rare person who switches these multiple personalities on and off at the flick of a mental switch. For most, a period of adjustment is necessary. In the car on the way to meet an aged parent, we compose ourselves and subconsciously go over things that we must or must not do when we arrive. Perhaps watching our language and avoiding swearing, for instance. We are, in effect, changing into another role: from adult to child.

There is an expression in anthropology which sums up neatly and concisely this essential aspect of commuting. The experience of travelling miles to and from one's home is an example of 'liminality', from the Latin *limen,* meaning a threshold. Liminality is the state of being between one thing and another. In a temporal sense, twilight is a liminal zone, lying as it does between day and night. In many rituals there are similar liminal regions, when one has ended one state of being, but not yet begun the next. This sums up commuting to a nicety. During the daily commute, one has left behind the world of home, but has not yet assumed the identity needed for the office. A transformation is about to take place and the commuting journey gives one time to adapt to this change and acclimatise to the necessary alteration in personality. The journey which we undertake to the office is not merely a physical one, from one geographical location to another; it is also a psychic transformation.

A beautiful description of this process is to be found in *Great Expectations,* when Wemmick, one of Dickens' walking commuters, explains to Pip the difference between his domestic character and that which he adopts once he reaches the office. Referring to his house fancifully as the 'castle', he says, 'The office is one thing, and private life is another. When I go into the office, I leave the castle behind me, and when I come into the castle, I leave the office behind me'. Later on, Wemmick expands upon this theme, telling Pip, 'Walworth is one place, and this office is another ... My Walworth sentiments must be taken at Walworth; none but my official sentiments can be taken in this office'. So it is with all commuters and their daily journeys are the cusp where those two separate lives intersect.

The theme of transformation and change works in diametric opposition to the other and more familiar part of commuting; the relentless sameness of the experience. Perhaps the most important feature of commuting is its predictability. One knows just which train will be caught and it is possible to gauge to the very minute when one will be arriving at work. Of course, in practice, this is not always the case and perhaps this accounts for the suppressed fury felt by so many commuters when an announcement is made over a loudspeaker that their usual train or Tube has been delayed. It throws all the most careful calculations out of kilter. It is instructive to observe the reactions of commuters on a platform of the London Underground in the morning, if they learn that some unfortunate soul has thrown himself in front of a train and so caused massive disruption to services. In the normal way of things, we are naturally aghast to learn of the death of a fellow human being and this is particularly so when the person concerned has been driven by personal misfortune to choose self-destruction over continued life. Commuters too, being only human, usually feel sympathy for a tragic event of this kind, but it is not uncommon to hear muttered imprecations under those circumstances, to the effect that committing suicide in such a way, especially at that time of day, is a monumentally selfish act. The fear of being late for work has eroded their humanity to the extent that the most important point about a death is that it will delay their arrival at work by a few minutes. This ties in also with the obsessive punctuality which has been a common feature among commuters for over 150 years.

The desire for a comfortable sameness in the journey to work extends to trivial things like always having a particular seat on the train to Town. Watching the people waiting on the platform of a suburban railway station at eight on a weekday morning, will reveal indications that many of them know each other by sight. This is usually only visible by all but invisible clues. Some might give a half nod of recognition, make brief eye contact or give a slight smile. They will seldom talk to each other though. When the train comes, their behaviour is like some highly ritualised dance. It is plain that most of them know where they will be sitting and there is an etiquette and code of behaviour which is fascinating to observe. They go through this same ritual every morning and it is clearly a satisfying and reassuring one to them, or they would not repeat it day after day.

It is while they are engaged in what is, on the face of it, a monotonous routine, that every one of those commuters will be undergoing a psychological change and in a sense becoming different people for the day ahead. In the evening, the process will be reversed and they will revert to their home personality.

There is one final point to consider about the twice-daily expeditions undertaken by commuters who use public transport and it is one which is so obvious that most fail altogether to notice it. Very few of us travel habitually by first class. On buses and Underground trains, there is of course no such thing and so we are crushed together with all the other travellers in one confined space. It took some decades for this sort of thing to become common practice when travelling to work. The first buses were, at least in theory, open to everybody of any class. In practice of course, because of their relatively high fares and the fact that they started running after most working men and women had already begun work; the passengers were almost exclusively middle class. Trams too were nominally open to all, but mostly used by working people.

In the next chapter, we shall be looking at London's Underground and discovering that the first real tube, the City and South London Railway, which opened in 1890, introduced the revolutionary idea of abolishing first, second and third class carriages, simply charging a flat rate of 2d (1p) for everybody. This was so cheap that manual workers as well as clerks flocked to travel on the new line. A natural consequence was that all classes of Victorian Britain found themselves jumbled together and sitting crowded cheek-by-jowl in cramped carriages. This was something of a novelty; company directors, commercial clerks, carpenters, labourers, seamstresses and shopgirls, all crowded together in one spot.

The result of all this mixing could not help but make the working and middle classes aware that they probably had more in common than they might previously have realised. It was impossible for a bank manager who travelled regularly on the same Tube train as group of labourers to pretend that they were really of a different order. It was patently obvious that they, like him, were going to work each day and that there were many other similarities as well.

Today, there are few external indicators of social class; it can be all but impossible to distinguish between a member of the upper middle class and somebody who works with his or her hands. In any case, the majority of people now believe themselves to be middle class, so such distinctions are, at least to some extent, meaningless. The modern-day equivalent of the social mixing with commuting by Tube promoted a century ago is based not upon class, but race. Despite living in such a multicultural society, most ethnic groups in Britain, including the white majority, still tend to stick together. Over 90 per cent of white people, for example, have no close friends belonging to an ethnic minority. Commuting on public transport is the one part of the day when this separation must, perforce, break down. Just as top-hatted Victorian businessmen found themselves sitting next to crossing sweepers on the morning Tube, so now do well-to-do City types end up sharing carriages on the Tube with black Rastafarians, covered Muslims, Orthodox Jews and Polish Catholics. The Tubes and buses are now, as they have been for many years, melting pots; where all manner of people come together.

Chapter 7

Beneath the Earth: The First Underground Trains

W e sometimes assume that congested city streets and gridlocks
are somehow associated with what used once to be referred to
facetiously as the 'infernal combustion engine'. In other words, it
looks to us today as though cars are the root cause of traffic problems in British
cities and that if a magic wand could be waved and all the petrol driven vehicles
made to vanish in the twinkling of an eye, then our streets would become
pleasant and relaxing places to be. Nothing could be further from the truth
and a quick look at the situation in the capital during the High Victorian period
of the mid-nineteenth century will show us why.

In June 1855, the Parliamentary Select Committee on Metropolitan
Communications was sitting in London. They hoped to find some radical
way of easing the chronically clogged condition of London's streets. Joseph
Paxton, designer of the Crystal Palace, Liberal MP and one of the foremost
architects of the day, was summoned to give evidence about the nature of the
problem. Paxton told the committee that it was quicker to travel by train from
Brighton to London Bridge Station than it was to go through London by road
from London Bridge to Paddington Station. Now *that's* congestion!

Of course, all the traffic on the roads at that time was drawn by horses and
much of it was commercial; carts delivering fresh produce, brewers' drays,
wagonloads of hay to feed the horses stabled in London and a hundred other
kinds of horse and cart carrying out the routine and commonplace tasks
associated with a city of more than two million inhabitants. A large part of the
problem, though, was caused by commuters.

The omnibuses introduced in 1829 by George Shillibeer had proved to be
phenomenally popular, so much so that the frantic competition had driven
him to bankruptcy in less than two years. There had been various attempts to
restrict and regulate the number of buses operating in London, but by 1850
there were over 1,300 in London. Until 1832, the centre of London had been
the exclusive preserve of Hackney Carriages, but when this ban had been lifted,
the West End and City of London soon became full of omnibuses, most of

them carrying people to work. Nor were buses the only method of road transport being used by London commuters that were clogging up the roads at that time.

There had been carriages for hire in London since the middle of the seventeenth century. The first Hackney Carriage licences were being issued in 1662; just after the restoration to the throne of Charles II. These vehicles were cumbersome and needed more than one horse to draw them. In 1834, just four years before Victoria came to the throne, a new, lightweight carriage for hire was invented. Joseph Hansom, an architect from York, devised and patented a two-wheeled cab which could be drawn by a single horse and was especially manoeuvrable; a vital quality when moving through the London traffic. It also had a very low centre of gravity, which made what became known as the Hansom cab, much less prone to overturning on tight corners than other carriages of the day. A Hansom cab may be seen in Illustration 13.

The Hansom cab was similar to, but not precisely the same as, a modern taxi. They were regularly used for short journeys across town on an *ad hoc* basis, but also became popular with the better-off type of City businessman, the kind of man who would not dream of sitting crammed cheek-by-jowl in one of the new omnibuses. For men such as this, the Hansom was a boon and soon became an established part of the commuting scene. In Chapter 3, we met Mr Bultitude, who lived in Paddington and had his office in Mincing Lane, in the City. Mr Bultitude frequently commuted to his office in a Hansom cab; so regularly in fact that he and the cab driver knew each other by name. This was no uncommon thing among men who were too grand to use buses, but could not quite afford to maintain their own carriages. The Hansom was the perfect compromise, which enable such important men to travel to work in privacy and comfort.

In addition to the Hansoms, there were four-wheeler carriages for hire, which were also used by the wealthier commuters. These were known as 'Growlers'. In 1886, 7,000 licenses were issued in London for Hansoms and another 4,000 for Growlers. It was these, in addition to the many buses that were making it such a time-consuming and frustrating task to make one's way across central London at that time.

The solution to the problem of the London traffic was simple and radical. It was to transport all those thousands of commuters away from the streets entirely and to whisk them from point to point in the city as though on a magic carpet which would not further contribute to the unbearably crowded conditions which obtained on the surface. This magic carpet, instead of flying over the roof-tops, would instead dive beneath the cellars and carry hundreds of people at a time in and out of the City and from one railway terminus to another.

Since the 1830s, Charles Pearson, the Member of Parliament for Lambeth, had been tirelessly promoting a scheme for building a railway line beneath the streets of London. His first idea was that a line might be constructed between the railway stations at King's Cross and Farringdon Street. If built by the 'cut and cover' method, the only one which could be envisaged at that time, such a line would have the further advantage of sweeping away many of the slums along the Fleet Valley. It would then be possible to lay a grand new road, wider than any already existing in London.

Before going any further, it might be an idea to explain briefly the two methods used for building the tunnels necessary for underground trains. The technology for tunnelling deep underground had not yet been developed when the first lines were built, at least not through the sloppy sea of clay upon which London sits. Tunnelling through rock is another matter entirely. There were fears that burrowing beneath buildings might have the effect of undermining their foundations and causing subsidence. Such deep-level 'tubes' were to be a later development. The method used for the first of the lines entailed cutting a very deep trench, which was open to the sky, and then building a roof over this upon which a road could be laid. The present-day Marylebone Road and Euston Road were both lie above the line of London's first underground railway. This method was known, for obvious reasons, as 'cut and cover'.

In 1846 a Royal Commission began to examine in detail many new proposals for railways in London. Pearson and his supporters thought that the time had come and he presented his plan for the underground line across the Fleet Valley. Like most people, the satirical magazine *Punch* was very sceptical about the practicality of such an enterprise and reported on Charles Pearson's presentation to the Royal Commission by saying that;

A survey has already been made and that many inhabitants along the line have expressed their readiness to place their coal cellars at the disposal of the company. It is believed that much expense may be saved by taking advantage of areas, kitchens and coal holes already made, through which the trains may run without much inconvenience to the owners, by making a judicious arrangement of the timetable. It will certainly be awkward if a family should be waiting for a scuttle of coals, and should not be able to get it until after the train has gone by; but a little domestic foresight, seconded by railway punctuality, will obviate all annoyances of this kind.

The Royal Commission rejected the idea of an underground railway and it was to be another four years before Pearson and his backers obtained permission to start work. Even then, Bills needed to be presented and passed through Parliament and it was not until January 1860 that the first shaft was sunk at Euston Square.

Inevitably, the western end of the new line was to be at Paddington. Readers might have noticed that Paddington and the adjacent district of Bayswater have featured in both the real-life development of commuter transport and also in the accounts of commuters in Victoria novels. Walter Hancock's steam buses ran from Paddington to the City of London, as did Shillibeer's first omnibuses in 1829. Paddington was the smartest residential suburb in London at that time and it made sense to bring the advantages of a new method of getting to work in the morning to those who needed and could afford to pay for such things. Paul Bultitude, the protagonist of *Vice Versa*, lived near Paddington Station and Mr Pooter's son moved to Bayswater because he thought Holloway to be a bit 'off'. When another public transport system was set up, Paddington must have seemed the logical place to begin.

Not that the underground railway was intended for the use only of those in the smarter districts. There is good reason to suppose that Charles Pearson's motives were, at least in part, philanthropic. When he was lobbying for the construction of the new railway, Pearson explicitly referred to the beneficial effects that the introduction of public transport in the form of buses had had on the middle class, to which he belonged. He said: 'I have seen the advantage to my own class. Sixpence takes us by omnibus backwards and forwards; the poor man has not sixpence to give; he has no leisure to walk, and no money to ride; he is chained to his scene of labour and there he must stay.' In private conversation, Charles Pearson advocated the creation of garden suburbs for the working classes, from which they could commute each day into the centre of London. Of course, this might all have been mere cant, disguising a brilliant business opportunity by representing it as an act of altruistic, social engineering. Subsequent events militate against a cynical view of the sort.

It took Pearson fourteen years to raise enough money to begin work on the Metropolitan Railway. Of the £300,000 which he managed to obtain, a good part was from the Corporation of London. As the line neared completion, the Metropolitan Company which he had helped create, offered him a reward for all his services. Charles Pearson, who in addition to everything else was the official solicitor to the City of London, refused, on the grounds that 'I am the servant of the Corporation of London; they are my masters, and entitled to all my time and service. If you have any return to make you must make it to them.' These hardly sound like the words of a businessman concerned only with personal profit!

Whatever Charles Pearson's motivations, his underground railway was of great benefit to working-class commuters. Like all railways at that time, tickets were sold as first, second or third class. Surprisingly, over 70 per cent of the tickets sold during the first few weeks of the Metropolitan Railway's operation were third class. The working classes were, from the very beginning, exceedingly keen on the Underground. So for that matter was everybody else in London; judging at least by the incredible numbers of passengers who used it. On Saturday, 10 January 1863, the first day that the new railway was open to the general public, 38,000 people rode on the new line. In the first year that it was in service, the Metropolitan Railway carried nine and a half million passengers. The following year, the number rose to twelve million, and this in a city which, according to the census of 1861, contained fewer than three million people! In keeping with Charles Pearson's vision, workmen's trains ran on the Metropolitan Railway from the start, one each way from Paddington to the city and back again. The first ran very early in the morning and the second in the evening. The fare was 1d each way; which was a sixth of what the bus fare would have been over the distance.

Once one underground railway had been built and become a roaring success, it was perhaps inevitable that more would follow. The District and Circle Lines were next, also constructed by the cut-and-cover method. It was to be a little while before proper 'tube' lines were begun, there being certain technical difficulties to overcome first. One of these was the need for a quick, safe and convenient method for digging what amounted to a mine through the clay which lies below London. Another was the problem of getting passengers down to the platforms of a deep line and then back up to the surface again at the other end. Lifts were installed and then, from 1911 onwards, escalators.

Cut-and-cover tunnels caused considerable disruption and were unsatisfactory in a number of ways. Some of the disadvantages of these early excavations still reverberate down the centuries and are visible to this day. One of the great problems when running steam trains underground is what to do with all the steam and smoke, which must regularly be vented from the engines. Because the trains were running very close to the surface, it was found that leaving at intervals an area open to the sky provided a neat solution. As the driver came to these parts of the line, he could open the relevant valves without running the risk of asphyxiating his passengers. In rougher neighbourhoods, this was not a great problem, the occasional plumes of smoke and jets of steam being taken in their stride by the inhabitants of working-class districts. All that was needed was to demolish a few houses and leave an open gap, where the railway line was visible. It was another thing entirely when the Metropolitan Railway wished to extend west, through Bayswater to South Kensington. One of the scheduled 'gaps', where the tunnel roof was left off, was at Leinster Gardens in Bayswater and the residents of this select neighbourhood had no intention at all of seeing the elegant façade of their row of townhouses being broken with an ugly space, showing a railway line.

The negotiations went on for some time, but the compromise which was in the end reached satisfied both parties and left as its legacies one of the most famous curiosities in London. Numbers 23 and 24 Leinster Gardens were indeed demolished to make way for the open section of track needed by the railway. However, two dummy houses were constructed in the empty space, to fit in with the other properties in the street. They stand there to this day, like some huge and utterly convincing stage set. Dummy houses, with false doors and painted windows, indistinguishable from all the other houses in the street until you get up close to them. In fact they are just facades, front walls and nothing more. They may be seen in Illustration 14.

Another flaw in the cut-and-cover method retained the potential to cause a disaster as late as the very end of the twentieth century, at midnight on 31 December 1999. The grassy area at the heart of Parliament Square has in recent years become something of a stage for political protestors, who have on occasion pitched tents there. What few of them realise is that only a thin crust separates them from the tunnels of the Circle and District Lines below. For several years before the celebration of the Millennium, engineers from London Transport had been growing uneasy about people walking across the grass of Parliament Square. Every so often, plans would be mooted for a monumental fountain or statue to be erected in the middle of the grass, but so thin was the layer between the grass and the railway line beneath, that nothing had come of such plans. For three years, the grass had been surrounded by fences, but it was known that thousands of people intended to celebrate the dawning of the new century by congregating in Parliament Square to hear the chimes of Big Ben at midnight. A major civil engineering project was undertaken in October 1999, during which the turf was removed from the square and a load-bearing platform installed. The area was then grassed over again and the crowds who gathered there on the night of 31 December 1999 were able to do so in perfect safety.

From time to time, efforts are made to improve conditions on the London Underground. These principally relate to cooling or freshening the air in the tunnels and on the platforms. In 2006, temperatures rose to 47 degrees Celsius on some platforms. Although it is customary to complain about such conditions, they are nothing at all compared to those which early passengers on the underground had to endure. From the beginning, it was obvious that there would be problems in running steam trains underground. Anybody who has seen a steam engine in operation will know that they generate clouds of steam and smoke, which in the normal way of things are able to dissipate into the open air. How would that work though in a continuous tunnels?

There were experiments with smokeless steam engines, but these were singularly unsuccessful. One idea was that it might be possible to heat bricks up and then use them to generate steam during the passage underground. A prototype of such an engine was built but it was a failure.

We saw above that open spaces were provided to allow the engines to release the steam which had built up in their condensing chambers, but it was not possible to contain the smoke from the engine, even temporarily. By using coke, rather than coal, the smoke and fumes could be reduced, but it was still pretty unpleasant in the tunnels of the first underground system. Commuters certainly patronised the underground in their millions from the moment that it was opened, but they needed great powers of endurance to do so. When Charles Pearson was giving evidence to the Royal Commission in 1846, one of the reservations expressed about his projected underground railway was that the passengers might all be suffocated by the fumes from the engines. This didn't happen, but there were ill effects for passengers. A journalist for *The English Illustrated Magazine* travelled in the cab of one of the locomotives pulling trains on the Circle Line in the early 1890s and his account makes fascinating reading. As soon as the train began to move, he wrote that, 'The sensation was altogether like the inhalation of gas preparatory to having a tooth drawn'. As the journey progressed, the atmosphere in the tunnels grew worse.

> The road now began to go uphill and at the same time the air grew more foul. From King's Cross to Edgware Road the ventilation is defective, and the atmosphere is on a par with the ''tween decks, forrud' of a modern ironclad in bad weather, and that is saying a good deal. By the time we reached Gower Street I was coughing and spluttering like a boy with his first cigar.
>
> 'It is a little unpleasant when you ain't used to it:' said the driver, with the composure born of long usage, 'But you ought to come here on a hot summer day to get the real thing!'

The comparison of the atmosphere with the gas used to anesthetise dental patients is revealing. At that time, nitrous oxide, more commonly known as 'Laughing Gas', was the gas used in dentistry. There were serious concerns about the levels of pollution in the tunnels of the Metropolitan and District lines and during the 1890s, chemists from the newly-formed London County Council took samples on the platforms of the Underground. They found that levels of sulphur were dangerously high, which was perhaps no surprise, given the amount of coal being burned underground. They also found unacceptably high levels of another hazardous substance, which was none other than nitrous oxide! The reporter who had been reminded by the smell of a trip to the dentist had been absolutely right. Following these investigations, the first fans were introduced on the Underground, in an attempt to remove pollutants.

The first deep-level 'tube' in the world, and also the first major railway to be powered by electricity, was the City and South London Railway, which opened to the public on 18 December 1890, running from King William Street in the City, under the Thames and then to Stockwell. Like all pioneering and experimental projects, there were teething difficulties with the new deep-level electric railway. The company had set up their own power station, but had grossly underestimated the amount of electricity which would be needed to run several trains simultaneously along miles of track. Because of the depth of the new 'tube', it had been known all along that it would be unrealistic to expect patrons to walk up to street level when they left their trains and so lifts were installed. These worked not by electricity but by hydraulic power, water pressure being the key to their operation. We are used to being whisked up and down by lifts today, but in 1890 it was a great novelty and people regarded travelling by lift as an experience in itself. A reporter from the *Daily News* wrote: 'The sensation of descending the lift 50 feet to get below the level of the Thames is somewhat similar to a balloon experience. In a balloon the earth seems to be sinking below you. In the King William Street lift, the world seems to be gently rising, the passenger all the while being pleasantly stationary.'

Apart from the two important technical innovation of a deep tube with electric trains, the City and South London Railway was revolutionary in another way. All railways in Britain up until that time, had strict divisions of class; with passengers paying more according to whether they wished to travel in first or second class carriages. This enabled the middle and upper classes to avoid, quite literally, rubbing shoulders with working-class travellers, by sitting next to them. The new 'tube' line did away with all such distinctions, charging a flat rate of 2d (1p) a journey, with all passengers sharing the same carriage.

We are so used to sitting next to all sorts of people on buses and tubes, that the radical nature of the City and South London Railway's policy might not be immediately apparent. In theory at least, most buses were one class, although there were one or two exceptions. For example, seats on top were cheaper and tended to be used by working-class people. Trams were of course freely available to all, but in practice almost exclusively used by working-class men and women. Railways had always had demarcations, designed to keep different classes apart from one another. Here was a new idea indeed; that all commuters, of any social standing, should be expected to sit next to each other on their way to work.

One of the new ideas put into practice in the first real tube train failed to find favour with commuters using the line. The carriages and engines which were in use on the Metropolitan and District Railways were standard models which might be found anywhere on the railways which ran on the surface. For the first custom-built carriages of the new 'tube' though, a radical new design was tried. Surely, since these trains would be running deep beneath the surface for the whole time, there would be nothing at all to see from any windows? Why not do away with windows altogether then? The reasoning may have been sound, but these windowless carriages with padded upholstery rising to a height of five feet, ending in tiny ventilation slits, meant that passengers could not tell which station they were at. Guards at the end of each carriage were supposed to call out the names of the stations as the train arrived at them, but they frequently forgot to do so or, which was worse, announced the wrong station. The experiment of windowless carriages was abandoned, but not before they had acquired the nickname of 'padded cells'.

The London Underground is of course the oldest underground urban railway in the world, opening over thirty years before anything similar in any other city. Britain led the way in this idea throughout the whole of the nineteenth century, the idea being slow to catch on in the rest of the world. As a result, not only the oldest, but also the third oldest underground railway in the world are both to be found in British cities. The next two underground railways arrived in what was practically a dead heat in 1896. In that year, a Metro was opened in the Hungarian capital of Budapest and, very shortly afterwards, Glasgow's Subway began running in the second largest British city.

There had been difficulties with running steam trains on the underground railways of London, disposing of the smoke and steam being a major problem, which was never satisfactorily solved. In Glasgow, an ingenious means was used to obviate such problems. This was done by keeping the steam engines in one place, rather than sending them through tunnels. Actually, the idea was not a new one, having first been tried, unsuccessfully in London, over twenty-five years earlier.

The City and South London Railway was the world's first real tube line with trains powered by electricity. There had, however, been an earlier tube, which instead of trains had used little trolley cars a bit like trams. In February 1869, a tunnel began to be excavated beneath the River Thames at Tower Hill. It would carry passengers across the river to the vicinity of London Bridge

Station and would, it was thought, be a great boon for commuters arriving at London Bridge who might wish to be swiftly transported to the City if London.

It took eighteen months to dig the tunnel and install the necessary machinery. At either end of the 1,350-foot tunnel were 4 HP steam engines, which both provided the motive power for the lifts which brought the passengers up and down and also pulled the miniature carriages backwards and forward. Each little tramcar could hold just twelve people, who paid a penny second class and twopence first class to cross under the river. The only advantage to buying a first class ticket was that one had priority in boarding the carriages. The modest fares charged and the extremely limited capacity of the Tower Subway soon proved to be uneconomical to run. The first passengers were carried through the Tower Subway on 2 August 1870, along the 2ft 6in gauge rails, but by the end of the year; the company had become bankrupt. It had been an ingenious idea and is regarded by some as the first tube line in the world.

The Tower Subway still had a role to play in bringing commuters into the City, despite its closure as a railway line. The rails were removed, along with the steam engines and lifts. Spiral staircases were put in and gas lighting laid on in the tunnel itself. Then, the place reopened as a pedestrian link between the working-class districts of Bermondsey and Deptford with the City of London. At only ½d a time, 20,000 people a week were soon crossing the Thames by the new subway. The vast majority of the million customers a year were working men and women who had previously been wholly reliant upon ferries.

So it was that for the next twenty-two years, the Tower Subway was a main route for working-class commuters to travel to and from their workplaces. It might have been cheap, but even so, 7d (3p) a week was still the equivalent of an hour or two's wages for a working man and when Tower Bridge opened in 1894, it sounded the death-knell for the subway. The bridge, which was a couple of hundred yards downriver from the Tower Subway, charged no toll to cross and the subway's income dropped overnight to almost nothing and it closed shortly afterwards.

The Glasgow District Subway, which opened on 14 December 1896, was a clutch-and-cable system, run in a similar way to the Tower Subway. An external steam plant powered two continuously moving steel cables, which ran on a circular route. The two cables were moving in opposite directions. Trains were equipped with cable-gripper mechanisms, which mean that to start moving, the driver caused the gripper to clasp the moving cable. Stopping at a station meant simply releasing the hold on the moving cable. There was no mechanism for allowing the carriages to go around the circuit a second time once they had arrived at the terminal and so they were simply lifted by crane to the other track and began travelling again in the opposite direction.

Perhaps because of the peculiar method of propulsion used in the early years of its existence, no attempt was ever made to extend the Glasgow Subway and it is still limited to the original route and stations which were opened well over a century ago.

Underground railways for commuters have never really caught on, except in London. In 1980, a light railway system which ran partly under the cities of Newcastle and Gateshead opened. The Tyne and Wear Metro is, however, the only such railway in Britain, apart from the ones in London and Glasgow. Perhaps it is simply that London is so big and the streets so crowded, that it makes sense to travel under, rather than through them, if possible. Elsewhere, commuters find it more convenient to remain above ground.

Chapter 8

Electric Trams and Motor Buses: Commuting in the First Half of the Twentieth Century

For almost the whole of British history, travelling along roads was the most common, indeed for millennia the only, way of moving about the country. In the eighteenth century canals began to be dug for the movement of freight, but passengers were still carried, as they always had been, along roads. There was a radical change from the 1820s onwards, with the construction of railway lines. During the rest of the nineteenth century the swiftest way of getting about was by carriages pulled behind steam engines. This was how things stood at the end of the century. Indeed, it was not until the 1920s that the railways began to decline in importance for transporting people, being gradually eclipsed from that decade onwards by the rise of the internal combustion engine as a mean for propelling vehicles along roads, rather than rails. That other transport system which relied upon rails, the urban tram, also reached its greatest use and widest service at the same time.

We will look later in this chapter at the implication for commuters of the rise of motor vehicles and the simultaneous decline of rail transport, but first we must see how commuters were being created by builders and railway companies working sometimes in tandem and at other times independently. The growth of the larger British cities sometimes took place piecemeal along the edges and at other time was of a more wholesale nature; with entire suburbs being thrown up almost overnight. To see how this happened, and the way in which entire communities designed expressly for commuters sprang up like mushrooms, it might be useful to look in detail at one particular example of this process.

In the mid-nineteenth century, the village of Ilford lay seven miles from the centre of London and to the east of the village was agricultural land, miles of fields with only the occasional farmhouse to vary the bleak monotony of the flat Essex countryside. There had been some building for the wealthier type of commuter who would catch a train from Ilford Station, and we have seen how the Ilford brickfields had proved a good hunting ground for fossils. The population explosion which struck the area during the closing years of the nineteenth century and the opening years of the twentieth was truly astounding. Not that such an exponential rise in numbers was atypical for that time; the industrial cities of Britain had been growing in this way for decades. In 1871, 5,947 people were living in Ilford. By 1911, this had increased to 78,188. Almost all these new residents were commuters who had moved into the district, and the reason for this is not hard to find.

There were factories and workplaces in established villages and towns like Ilford, but they employed a relatively small number of local people. The huge estates which were soon to be built on the nearby fields included various amenities such as shops, schools, public houses and churches, but no additional places of employment for the tens of thousands of people who would be moving there. What happened was that a couple of square miles of open countryside would be marked out into a grid pattern of streets and the houses built. At the same time, parades of shops with flats above them would also be built, a certain number of shops for so many houses. Writing of this development in 1901, one observer remarked of the newly-built districts of Seven Kings and Goodmayes, deliberately planned suburbs on the edge of Ilford, as being a 'place which came suddenly into existence like a mushroom, and which became a town without going through the preliminary stage of hamlet and village'.

The new areas of housing were perfectly decent homes, but there was no history or growth to them; they came into existence fully-formed, with all the houses empty and waiting for occupants. In 1896, it was remarked by one local person that 'Ilford is the home of the smaller civil servant, the clerk and the young professional man'. It was, from the beginning of its establishment, a dormitory town for white-collar workers.

There is today something a little monotonous and depressing about these ready-made suburbs. Each street looks just the same as the next and even the rows of shops are identical. Every mile or two, there is a similar parade of shops. Perhaps this is one of the reasons that in the years following the end of the Second World War, many young people felt a revulsion towards the suburbs and suburban life. The average suburb which was erected around this time is certainly not an attractive and aesthetically pleasing environment, to say the least of it! It is little wonder really that *Private Eye* struck upon Neasden in the 1960s as symbolising all that the rising generation detested about suburban life.

The street names of the suburbs which were going up at the turn of the century can be revealing. In Seven Kings, one of the tracts of housing which covered the fields around Ilford, one notes Mafeking Avenue, Ladysmith Avenue and Kimberley Avenue, all in one little cluster. Seeing the names of famous engagements of the Boer War in this way allows us to date the construction of these streets to within a matter of months. Elsewhere, an attempt has been made to portray one of these stretches of drab suburban streets as being glamorous and wealthy. Half a mile to the north of Ilford Station, we find Kensington Gardens and Mayfair Avenue. One wonders if any of the minor civil servants or commercial clerks who moved into these streets were really deceived into believing that they were living in a part of London to rival the West End.

The street names listed above are interesting for the light which they shed upon the hopes and aspirations of what were described as the 'smaller civil servant, the clerk and the young professional man', those who would be moving into the newly-built houses in Kensington Gardens and Mayfair Avenue. These were people who wished to persuade themselves that they were moving out of the city entirely and into the countryside. It will be remembered that the earliest commuters during the Industrial Revolution actually moved into rural areas, the villages surrounding the growing cities such as Manchester and Birmingham. Perhaps for this reason, most of the streets being built on the edge of large cities, specifically for commuters, tended not to be called streets or roads. Instead, they were named 'avenue', 'gardens', 'lane' or 'park'. This snobbishness about the names of the streets in which commuters live still lingers on to this day. In the summer of 2015, a survey commissioned by Barclays Bank found that a property with 'lane' in its address sold on average for a fifth more than one in a 'road'. The cheapest homes were to be found in 'streets'!

The development of commuter suburbs like those of Ilford and the neighbouring districts of Seven Kings, Goodmayes and Chadwell Heath were deliberately undertaken with transport links in mind. The railway line from Liverpool Street to Romford was a lure for builders, even though there were not yet any stations for the men who would be buying the houses. The developer responsible for the building of Seven Kings and Goodmayes came to an arrangement with the Great Eastern Railway, offering them guarantees as to the number of commuters who would buy season tickets to use on their line, if they would only construct new stations to serve what had been, until a year or two earlier, just fields. The railway companies benefited from such deals, because once the stations had been built, thousands of new passengers began using the lines each day. In some new suburbs, the builders even threw in a season ticket to encourage potential purchasers.

Just as was to happen with the Metropolitan Railway and the new estates of what became known as 'Metro-land', the Great Eastern began to advertise the advantages of the areas where they had been persuaded to build the new stations. In 1911, the Great Eastern Railway published a brochure entitled *By Forest and Countryside*, which, considering that pretty much all the countryside along the side of the line had now been built on, was rather ironic. Readers learned that: 'Broad and pleasant roads and comfortable moderate sized houses run north and south from the old Roman highway. The whole area is built on a plain.' It is slightly surprising to see the fact that those 'moderate sized houses' were built on a plain, being advertised as some sort of advantage! To be more precise, much of the commuter housing in that area which had been thrown up in such frantic bursts of activity over the course of a few years was on a *flood* plain, along the banks of the River Roding. Shortly after they had been sold and the new occupiers had moved in, the grandly-named streets such as Kensington Gardens and Mayfair Avenue had been flooded, when the Roding burst its banks in 1903. There had been a good reason why nobody in the preceding centuries had thought to build their homes on that spot; it was a flood meadow. This sort of problem proved not at all uncommon during the great booms in commuter housing, where speed of construction and swift sales were the chief consideration.

In British cities at this time, the quickest and most convenient method of travelling short distances was still by horse power. Buses and trams, however, were the best way of getting from the outskirts of a city to its centre and back again. Unless you were fortunate enough to live in either London or Glasgow, with their underground railways, horse-drawn buses and trams were the usual mode of transport for short journeys. All this was to change dramatically in the early years of the twentieth century and commuters were in the forefront of the changes which took place. One of the alterations which the new century brought was that roads gradually began to be reclaimed for long-distance travel. This was of course due to the development of efficient and reliable internal combustion engines. The other thing which was seen in the field of transport in the early years of the twentieth century, which was connected in part with the rise of motor vehicles, was the rapid decline in the use of horses for transport.

In the 1880s, commuting in Britain was heavily reliant upon horses, a pair of which pulled every bus and tram. It was by that time becoming fairly clear though that the dependence upon horses was in many ways more trouble than it was worth. Simply maintaining the many horses used for public transport had grown into a vast industry. A few figures will illustrate this point. In London alone, 50,000 horses kept the buses and trams running. Each horse, whether pulling a tram or a bus, could only work for three or four hours at a stretch before needing to be changed for a fresh animal. In other words, every fifteen miles or so, buses and trams had to halt while the horses were changed. This necessitated a network of stables across the capital. Most of these have vanished, but one or two still remain. Horses seldom worked singly and to keep one bus or tram on the road for a working day required no fewer than twelve horses.

Of course, all those horses had to be stabled and looked after while they were not working and this was a huge undertaking. There were vets, blacksmiths and farriers to pay, to say nothing of the staff responsible for keeping the stables in order and the huge amounts of feed needed. The city streets were hard on the feet of horses and they required frequent shoeing. In London alone, the annual bill for horseshoes at the turn of the century for the London General Omnibus Company was £20,000. Even so, there didn't, until the late 1880s, appear to a viable alternative for the reliance upon horses for commuter transport.

An event on the other side of the Atlantic gave a clear warning of the dangers of allowing urban life to remain so heavily dependent upon the use of horses. In the autumn of 1872, an epidemic of equine influenza began in the Canadian province of Ontario. From there, it spread first to other parts of Canada and then across the border into the United States. This disease caused horses to develop symptoms similar in many ways to the influenza which afflicted humans. The creatures became listless and feverish, being racked by violent fits of coughing. For a week or two, horses suffering from this particularly virulent strain of equine influenza were quite unable to carry riders, pull carts or undertake any sort of exertion. Between 1 per cent and 10 per cent of them died of the illness. Of course, farming ground to a halt in areas where the epidemic raged, but the effects in the cities of North America were if anything even worse. The movement of goods in and around cities ground to a halt, as 95 per cent of the horses in an area fell ill. Fire engines were unable to tackle emergencies, the barges which carried heavy goods in and out of cities could not move, no deliveries of milk or food could be made, and of course, all trams and buses stopped running. In New York alone, over 20,000 horses sickened in the course of a single week. The 'Great Epizootic', as it became known, was a wakeup call for those who relied altogether upon horses. While it lasted, some desperate companies tried hitching oxen to pull trams; others even resorted to gangs of men. None of it was any use though and the events of 1872 demonstrated in the starkest way imaginable the risks of depending upon horses to keep a modern city running.

After the Great Epizootic was over, a frantic search began for ways to reduce dependence upon horses alone for the transport systems of American cities. Steam-powered trams were one experiment, but steam locomotives were not really suitable for busy city streets. Cables running from a fixed power plant were another method tried and these were somewhat more successful for powering trams. San Francisco became the first city to install a practical arrangement of cable cars and Chicago and Denver followed suit. Then, in the 1880s, inventors turned to electricity as a possible way of running trams. As will be recalled, British cities first began allowing trams to run in the early 1870s and they were granted, by Act of Parliament, an initial 21-year lease before local authorities were given the option of taking them over and running the tram for themselves. As the years ticked towards the end of the leases, municipal authorities in Britain where horse-drawn tramways were carrying working-class commuters out to the suburbs, watched with great interest the experiments being made abroad. The European cities of Berlin, Frankfurt and Brussels, as well as Baltimore and Cleveland across the Atlantic, all set up electrically-powered tramways. All were miserable failures. By 1887, ten such lines had been operating. Not one made a profit.

The chief difficulty with these early electric trams was that the power was being delivered to the motors in the vehicles via the rails on which they were running. This was dangerous, causing the electrocution of dogs and cats, and also the current leaked away, causing water pipes to corrode. It was not until 1887 that the electricity began to be carried in overhead wires. This was the method used in the first commercially-successful electric tramway in Richmond, Virginia. A spring-loaded trolley pole connected the tram with the wires. The way was now open to convert the trams carrying commuters in British cities from horse power to electricity. The first electric tram to run in Britain, at Northfleet in Kent in 1889, may be seen in Illustration 15.

Before looking at the implications of the new type of trams for commuting in this country, a few words might be in order about the advantages of electric trams; apart from the most obvious one, that is, that they ended the need to maintain tens of thousands of horses in city stables. Keeping weight to an absolute minimum had always been a major consideration when manufacturing tram cars. Because they were drawn by just two horses and were expected to carry many passengers, the structure of the tram was kept as light as possible. Wood was used in preference to metal and solid parts were frequently made ornately with trelliswork and decorative holes just in order to reduce the weight. This might have been the case with just two horses pulling a tram, but the electric motors installed in those early electric trams were extremely powerful, 75 horsepower being not uncommon. This meant that weight was no longer a consideration when building tramcars or calculating how many passengers could be carried in them. Indeed, the more weight, the better the traction. When two horses were pulling a tram, one always had to be strict about the number of people that could be in the carriage; with the equivalent of seventy-five horses pulling the thing, this became an irrelevance. Not only could the carriages be made from cast iron and with extravagant and heavy flourishes, it was also possible to allow as many standing passengers to ride as could find room. Suddenly, trams could service a greater area of the outer suburbs than was previously the case.

The municipal authorities in Britain's larger cities almost invariably took over the tramlines when the leases expired and all made plans to change over from horse-drawn vehicles to electricity. At the same time, the opportunity was seized to create many more working-class commuters. This was a deliberate policy on the part of local government to engage in a massive programme of social engineering.

These days, the expression 'social engineering' is invariably used in a pejorative and disapproving way. When some policy, relating perhaps to universities or schools, is described as being 'social engineering'; we know that we are invited to dismiss it as a piece of Stalinist and statist interference in the natural order of things. It was not always so. Until 1889, there was no unitary local authority for the whole of London. Outside the City of London, there were only individual parishes and boroughs. In 1889, the London County Council was established and very soon gave thought to how best the dreadful slums of the East End and Central London could be dealt with and improved. The obvious, indeed the only, solution, was to disperse the inhabitants outwards, into the suburbs of London and the countryside around those suburbs. Eventually, this theory of encouraging the migration of working-class people away from the central areas was to reach its zenith in the creation of the world's biggest public housing project at Becontree in Essex, but to begin with, the aims were slightly more modest.

The first step in getting people to move further out of London would be to ensure that they would be able to come back into Town to work. If there was a cheap and reliable form of public transport between the inner areas of London and the countryside of Hertfordshire and Essex, then this would act as a network of capillaries which would naturally draw people away from the slums and out towards the suburbs. If combined with relatively modest housing projects which would provide the nuclei of new communities, then the process would tend, as a matter of course, to accelerate and working people would cheerfully leave the East End slums and move to places such as Enfield and Waltham Cross, neither of which were at that time in London. Similar schemes were being contemplated in other cities such as Birmingham and Manchester.

The motive power for this exodus would be provided by new electric trams, operated in the capital by the London County Council. In the years before the outbreak of the First World War, a huge expansion of the old horse-drawn tramlines took place, until it was possible to travel over the whole of London and large parts of the Home Counties by electric tram. Much the same thing was happening in the industrial cities of the Midlands, Northern England and Southern Scotland. The electric tram became the preferred means of travel for working men and women across the whole of Britain.

The decision to do away with horses on the trams was pretty much a planned and conscious one, but the end of horse-drawn buses was more a natural consequence of the laws of economics. Nobody set out to rid the country of horse-drawn buses: they simply withered away as the advantages of the new motor buses revealed themselves. The *Bradford Observer* carried in its edition of 25 September 1897, the following advertisement:

The Yorkshire Motor Co Ltd, Albert Hall, Bradford.
Motor omnibuses daily from Town Hall to Four Lane Ends

The new service was offered by James Edward Tuke, who was a motor agent in Harrogate and Bradford. Mr Tuke was evidently something of a mover and shaker in the emerging world of the internal combustion engine, because less than a year earlier, In December 1896, he had begun one of the world's first car-hire firms, renting out two-seater Arnold Sociables for three shillings an hour.

Surprisingly, it took almost two years for the idea of motor buses to spread from Bradford to London. The first scheduled motor bus service in London was inaugurated on 9 October 1899, by the Motor Traction Company. It ran from Kennington to Victoria, via Westminster Bridge. In no time at all, the motor bus in London was transformed from an intriguing novelty to an integral part of everyday life. The rise of the petrol engine was a recognised phenomenon across the whole country in the years preceding the First World War; with buses and other commercial vehicles leading the way. For commuters, the tipping point in this respect was reached on 31 October 1910. On that day, the rising numbers of motor buses met the declining horse buses and there were 1,142 of each licensed in London. The writing was on the wall though for horse buses and less than four years later, on 4 August 1914, the last one in London made the journey from Peckham. In one or two provincial towns, horse-drawn buses lingered on; but for commuters wishing to use public transport, the choice was now between steam trains, electric trams, the 'Tube' and motor buses.

The roads really belonged now to the internal combustion engine and it was this which carried more and more commuters, firstly by bus and then, later in the century, by car. Before we look at the inexorable rise of the private motor vehicle though, we might see how the electric trams went the way of the horse-drawn buses. In the years leading up the First World War, the electric tram appeared to be unstoppable as the chief means of commuting for the working classes, so much so that the Chief Officer of the London County Council Tramways was able to suggest in 1909 that within twenty years, motor buses would be relegated to the position of curiosities in museums. Everywhere one looked in Britain, the electric tram was triumphant. We have seen that the chief industrial regions of Britain were in South Wales, roughly from Swansea to Newport, in the Midlands around Birmingham, Coventry, Dudley and Wolverhampton, in Stoke-on-Trent, the north of England, including Liverpool, Manchester, Bradford and Sheffield, the North-East, with Newcastle and Middlesbrough, and of course Southern Scotland, around the Clyde. A look at the electric tramways running before the First World War shows us their importance.

After the leases granted to private companies to run tramways in British cities expired in the 1890s, municipal authorities took over their running. About the turn of the century, all such systems were electrified. Looking at a map showing the towns and cities with extensive tram systems, those suitable for carrying commuters, shows that they were restricted to industrial areas such as Liverpool, Birkenhead, Manchester, Salford, Stockport, Wigan, Bradford, Blackburn, Huddersfield, Sheffield, Birmingham, Stoke-on-Trent, Newcastle and Glasgow. The electric tram was the perfect way of transporting workers to factories and then returning them to their homes at the end of the day.

London too had a very large system of trams, which ran across the whole of the city, with of course the exception of the West End and the City of London. One might have thought that electric trams were here to stay, but in fact almost from the beginning, they were unable to compete with the new motor buses. In retrospect, the explanation for this is not hard to understand. Setting up trams requires an enormous capital outlay before a single passenger has been carried. Rails must be laid, electrical cables must be strung up on standards which have been erected, vehicles built, roads adapted; the list is a long one. Once you have done this, it is true that numbers of passengers can be very great. In London, 800 million passengers were carried by trams in just one year in 1914. That is almost a billion people taken to and fro, generating a very large amount of money even taking into account the modest fares charged. Even so, by the 1920s, the trams of London were losing money. It was not that there was less demand for them, but simply that the costs associated with the maintenance and generation of power were rising steadily. Keeping the rails in good order and repairing them was a large part of this expense. Local authorities were being faced with a stark choice. Either they could raise their rates, which were the equivalent of the present-day Council Tax, or they could dismantle and abandon their tramways. Raising the rates was never popular and so there was a strong inclination to give up trams.

There was another reason why the days of the trams were over. When your streets are filled only with a few horses and carts or buses, then there is no problem in allocating the central part of a roadway to the rails along which the trams passed. With more and more cars and lorries appearing on the streets though, that area given over to the tramlines was beginning to cause traffic problems. Since an ever greater number of commuters were switching to the use of buses in any case, perhaps it was thought that the trams were simply an unnecessary duplication of the existing, and perfectly adequate, bus routes.

Talking of duplication of bus routes reminds us that so great was the enthusiasm for electric trams in the early years of the twentieth century, that it was seriously suggested that in London they could rival the Tube. Plans were laid for a network of shallow cut-and-cover tunnels across London, which would enable trams to travel underground across the whole of the city from Holloway in the north to the Elephant and Castle in the south. In 1905 the London County Council put forward a scheme to the Royal Commission on London Traffic, which would have seen the building of a four-mile tram tunnel to link Knightsbridge with the City of London. The fact that such a tunnel, as well as the others suggested, would have simply replicated the Underground caused the Royal Commission to reject the idea. In the end, only a short tunnel for trams to run underground was built. This fragment of an unrealised dream still exists beneath Kingsway, running from near Holborn Tube station down to the Aldwych.

Faced with a loss-making enterprise, the municipal trams at first did what anybody would under such circumstances, which was to raise prices. This had the inevitable effect of driving even more people to use the cheaper motor buses for their journeys to work. In London, by 1923, more people were using buses than trams and by 1930, buses were carrying twice as many passengers as the London trams. The writing was on the wall and led to the closure of the tramways and their replacement with another electric vehicle, one which was for a while very popular with commuters: the trolleybus.

Trams may have been struggling to survive in competition with buses during the 1920s, but an awful lot of working people still used them. In 1928, 4,706 million journeys were made by tram. Their decline was part of a general falling-out of favour of rail transport. As cars, buses and lorries became commoner, travellers tended to use these rather than trains or trams. The peak of the railways was reached in 1914, when there was over 21,000 miles of track in Britain and the railways were employing around three quarters of a million people. From that high point, it was a picture of slow decline for rail systems generally. The writing was on the wall and led to the closure of the tramways and their replacement with another electric vehicle, one which was for a while very popular with commuters: the trolleybus.

The abandonment of trams in favour of trolleybuses took place all over Britain during the 1920s and 1930s. In London and Manchester, Birmingham and Glasgow, Newcastle and Bradford, trolleybuses were found to be a cheap and convenient alternative for the trams. The trolleybuses ran by electricity from overhead wires, just to trams, but there the similarity ended. Trams were restricted to metal rails set in the middle of the road. One consequence of this was that they were very noisy as they rattled their way along. They also tended to shake the passengers about rather. Because they ran on rubber wheels, like any other kind of bus, the trolleybuses gave a far smoother ride. The only noise which they generated was the quiet hum of their electric motors.

One of the things that people really liked about trolleybuses, as compared with trams, was that they did not have to dodge through traffic to board and leave them. Because trams travelled along rails, they could not of course pull into the kerb. Trolleybuses though could be steered. As long as they did not lose contact with the overhead wires from which they drew their power, they could pull up at the side of the road, just like any other bus.

There was one final advantage of the trolleybus over the tram, which was a psychological, rather than a practical one; they were actually buses! The tram had always been generally acknowledged to be a working class mode of commuting. This presented no problem as long as the millions of people using them were happy to be regarded as working class. This was the case throughout the nineteenth and well into the twentieth century. However, after the First World War, more and more people became reluctant to think of themselves as being working class. Until 1948, the majority of the population, just, described themselves when asked as working class, but since then the proportion has been declining every year. Today, fewer than 30 per cent of people asked in surveys, describe themselves as belonging to the working class. Most people now prefer to think of themselves as middle class.

In the 1920s and 1930s, as electric trams were becoming less and less profitable for local authorities to operate, this trend was gathering pace. Even factory workers did not like to believe that they belonged to the working class. The large-scale slum clearances which took place between the wars reinforced this sense of somehow becoming middle class. After all, these men and women were now living in suburbs, not crowded little streets in the inner cities. More than that, they had become commuters! True, they still had the same jobs as before, but now they lived in suburbs or semi-rural areas and travelled to work each day. This made them feel like respectable people, like bank clerks and accountants. The added expense of paying fares every day was a burden, but the increase in status often made up for this financial loss.

The only fly in this particular ointment was that travelling to work by tram marked these aspiring members of the suburban middle class out at once as being imposters. Only the working classes used trams. Since tram fares were rising anyway, as councils tried to make the system pay its way, quite a few working-class commuters switched to taking the bus to work instead. This became a vicious circle, as fewer and fewer people used the trams, they became increasingly unviable form a financial viewpoint.

The trolleybus solved all these various difficulties at a stroke. It meant, in the first instance, that there was no more track to be maintained. The new trolleybuses had a greater capacity than trams, being able to carry sixty or seventy passengers, rather than fifty. Best of all, there was none of the stigma attached to them from which the trams suffered. Buses were buses and one could not make any snap judgments about class, simply from observing who was using a trolleybus. You were as likely to encounter an bank manager as a foundry worker on a trolleybus.

The trends in public transport for commuters at which we have looked in this chapter, laid the way for the greatest revolution in commuting of all. People would of course still use buses, trains and tubes, but the main way of getting to work was already beginning to change. The internal combustion engine was to sweep all before it and it would not be long before public transport itself became an irrelevance for an increasing number of commuters. The age of the car was dawning. Today, of course, driving to work by car is the most popular form of commuting overall, beating all other methods combined.

Chapter 9

Lynching and Bombs: Death and the Commuter

Perhaps because of the perceived humdrum and routine nature of the lifestyle, sudden and violent death seems to be somehow antithetical to the whole idea of commuting. The commuter is a patient, industrious and reliable person, whose life is punctual, stable and wholly predictable. How shocking then that such a life should be cut short in the midst of the journey to work in the morning or while on the way home at night. Such deaths jar a little, because they do not fit in with how we expect the world to work. Murder, mayhem and disaster are the last things that one would associate with the peaceful custom of commuting to and from the City!

Of course, the occasional accident will in general pass without remark. One expects, after all, for mechanical contrivances such as buses, trains and trams to malfunction from time to time and the odd few deaths consequent upon such mishaps, while distressing enough for victims and their families, are not really all that shocking. The case is altered dramatically in the case of the intentional causing of death; the juxtapositioning of commuting and murder being a very rare and noteworthy event.

The random and individual deaths of commuters from violent attacks must surely have occurred from the very beginning of the practice of travelling miles into and out of the heart of a city in order to work. Men and women have been assaulted and killed en route to their place of work without anybody, other than the victims' immediate families, having taken any particular note of the occurrence. It was only with the use of public transport by commuters that such murders became in any way noteworthy, partly perhaps because of the very novelty of commuting by public transport. The first such death on a railway train was a shocking affair for the Victorians and is still remembered to this day. It was the subject of a popular book only a few years ago.

Those who travel by train, whether above or below ground, are so used to the sight of what were once known as 'communication cords', that they tend simply take them for granted as a natural and indispensable feature of any railway carriage or Tube train. Rather than a cord or chain, these days the system is more likely to consist of a bright red handle which may be operated in an emergency, making a light flash and a buzzer sound in the driver's cabin, When first installed though, these devices were directly connected to the brakes of the train and pulling them would cause a change in pressure in a vacuum tube and operate the brakes. This would in turn alert the driver to the fact that something was amiss.

Communication cords did not become widespread on British trains until about 1900, although the legislation which had required them to be fitted to trains had been passed over thirty years earlier, in 1868. That year saw the passing of the Regulation of Railways Act. This provided for, among other things, prosecution for trespassing on railway lines and the removal of fallen trees which might obstruct the track. One clause contained the following provision: 'Every company shall provide and maintain in good working order, in every train worked by it which carries passengers, and travels more than twenty miles without stopping, such efficient means of communication between the passengers and the servants of the company in charge of the train as the Board of Trade may approve.' Although the law at first merely stipulated that such a regulation would apply only to those trains which travelled for more than twenty miles without stopping, eventually every carriage in every train, including those on the Underground, was to be equipped with an emergency 'communication cord'. How this came about is an interesting story in itself, involving as it did the murder of a commuter which became something of a cause célèbre in Britain.

At ten past ten on the evening of Saturday, 9 July 1864, two men entered a first class carriage of a west-bound train on the North London Railway. They saw at once that the compartment was liberally splashed and besmeared with blood, suggesting that some act of violence had recently taken place in it. A guard was summoned and the alarm raised, but by this time the driver of another train had already spotted a gravely injured man laying by the tracks near Hackney Wick, in East London.

Thomas Briggs, the senior cashier at a City of London bank, had been beaten ferociously around the head and robbed of his gold glasses and watch. Mr Briggs lived in Hackney's Clapton Square and commuted each day to the City by railway. He died shortly after being found. At that time, there were no connecting corridors between individual compartments and so if anything untoward happened during a journey, there was no way of alerting anybody or calling for help. It was guessed that the inoffensive Mr Briggs, who was returning home from his work in the bank that day, had been attacked and then flung from the carriage while the train was travelling between stations.

There were few clues, other than a hat which did not belong to the dead man and the fact that Mr Briggs' gold watch and chain were missing, as well as his own hat.

Travelling by train in general, and commuting by rail in particular, were both increasingly common during the mid-1860s. Some people were nervous of using trains though, because once shut in a carriage with a stranger, there was no way of escaping if he proved to be dishonest or aggressive. Luggage thefts at stations had become prevalent, as had assaults on women and what we would now call muggings of lone travellers. This sort of thing typically happened when a would-be robber or molester of women found a single passenger alone in a compartment. This was evidently what had befallen Mr Briggs.

Nobody could provide any description of the man who had evidently shared Mr Briggs' compartment on the last journey home from work which he was destined to make. The only clue was the hat which had been found. Combined with the fact that Mr Briggs' own hat was missing, this led the police to suspect that for some reason the murderer had decided to swap hats with his victim. The crime was solved nine days after its commission by a curious event. A cab driver approached the police and said that he had a suspicion that a young German whom he knew slightly might have been involved in the by now famous railway murder. This man, a tailor called Franz Muller, had given the cab driver a gold chain for his pocket watch. It had been in a cardboard box bearing the name of a jeweller who ran a shop in central London. When the police visited the jeweller, they found that Muller had obtained the gold chain not by purchasing it, but by exchanging it for another. When officers examined this chain, they found that it was the one which had been taken from the murdered man's watch. The jeweller, John Death, identified Muller from a photograph.

All that was now necessary was to arrest the German, but this was easier said than done, because by the time a warrant had been issued, Franz Muller had left the country, heading for New York on the sailing ship *Victoria*. A police inspector succeeded in getting a passage on a steamship, which arrived in New York three weeks before the *Victoria*. Muller was arrested and found to be in possession of both Mr Briggs' watch and also his hat. He was extradited to stand trial in Britain.

The Old Bailey trial of Franz Muller for what was known as the 'Railway Murder' lasted for three days. Muller protested his innocence and the defence made much of the possibility that the cab driver who had first contacted the police might have done so only to claim the large reward being offered for information leading to the conviction of the banker's murder. It was to no avail and on 29 October 1864, the man responsible for the first murder on a British railway was sentenced to death.

It was to be another three-and-a-half years before the abolition of public executions in Britain and Franz Muller's hanging, which took place outside London's Newgate Prison on 14 November was a gruesome illustration of just why it was felt that public executions served no useful purpose in a modern, industrial society. The 50,000-strong crowd, which had been gathering all night, behaved with appalling levity. It was more like a street party than a solemn occasion which would culminate in a man's death. There was drunkenness, singing of comic songs, sexual activity and a general mood of coarse enjoyment. It was the awful nature of the sort of crowds which gathered to witness the spectacle of a public execution which was largely responsible for the move towards private hangings. On the scaffold, the Lutheran pastor who had attended Muller since he had been sentenced to death had one last exchange with him before the executioner did his work. He said afterwards that the prisoner's final words were 'Ich habe es getan', which translates roughly into English as, 'I did it'.

The first railway murder made many travellers uneasy and despite the various modifications made to trains to reassure lone passengers, such as communication cords and corridors between compartments, there was a wave of anxiety and public pronouncements by people to the effect that they would never again feel safe on a railway train. As is generally the case with such panics, it died down in time and had no long-term effects on the numbers using trains.

The murder of an inoffensive commuter like Mr Briggs caused a great deal of outrage and is still remembered to this day. A popular account of the case became something of a bestseller as recently as 2012. Whether it was because he belonged to a different class, being a manual worker rather than a well-to-do banker, or for some other reason, the murder of commuter Harry Pitts, which was committed some thirty years after that of Mr Briggs, has, by contrast, been entirely forgotten. This is odd, because in many ways the death of Harry Pitts was of far more relevance to the modern world than the simple beating to death of an elderly man for his watch and chain.

There is a popular and wholly mistaken belief that terrorism is somehow a modern scourge; one which has only emerged in the last thirty or forty years. Nothing could be further from the truth. When the so-called 7/7 attacks were carried out on London Tube trains in 2005, it was widely assumed that nothing of the sort had ever before been seen in the capital. In fact the first bomb attacks on commuters using the London Underground took place not in

2005, nor during the IRA campaigns of the 1970s, but in the reign of Queen Victoria.

The forerunners of the IRA were a group called the Irish Republican Brotherhood, otherwise known as the Fenians. In 1868 they were responsible for the greatest loss of life in a terrorist explosion in London prior to the 7/7 attacks, when fifteen men, women and children were killed by the detonation of a quarter of a ton of gunpowder in Clerkenwell. A few years later, a concerted bombing campaign was launched against targets in Britain ranging from a barracks in Manchester to the London police headquarters at Scotland Yard. One of the earliest of these attacks took place on the evening of Tuesday 30 October 1883.

Many commuters travelled home by Tube later than is now customary, working hours being in general longer than is the case today. At a few minutes past eight on that Tuesday, a Metropolitan Railway train had just left Edgware station, heading towards Paddington, when there was a terrific explosion; likened by some to a clap of thunder and by others to the sound of artillery. A bomb had exploded on the track as the westbound train passed it. By an eerie coincidence, the bomb went off at almost exactly the same spot as the bomb which was detonated on a train leaving Edgware for Paddington 122 years later when the Islamist suicide bombers struck in 2005.

Fortunately, nobody was killed by the explosion in the tunnel near Edgware station in the 1883 attack, although fifty people were injured by flying glass from the windows shattered by the blast. In another uncanny foreshadowing of the 7/7 attacks, a second bomb had been timed to explode simultaneously with the one at Edgware. This one went off in a tunnel on the District Line between Charing Cross and Westminster stations. The only injuries caused were to passengers standing on the platform at Charing Cross; some of whom were knocked over by the force of the explosion.

There was another explosion on the Tube on the evening of Friday 2 January 1885, when a bomb was detonated in the tunnel between King's Cross and Gower Street. The only casualties were a few cuts and scratches caused by broken glass. It was a miracle that none of those on the commuter trains targeted by the bombers in the 1880s had been killed. The reason was perhaps because the bombs had been planted on the track, rather than in the carriages themselves. The next bombing, which resulted in the first fatality in a terrorist bombing on London's Underground, differed from the Fenian attacks, in that those planting the device placed it inside the train.

At the end of the nineteenth century, there was great concern in Europe and America about the activities of fanatical terrorists who regarded the Western, democratic systems as being hopelessly decadent and corrupt. These militants aimed to destabilise various countries by acts of savagery, such as bombing railways stations and theatres. So fierce was the ideology motivating these ruthless men, that they appeared indifferent even to their own deaths, if these could serve the cause to which they had dedicated their lives. These were the Anarchists, and although Britain suffered less from their activities than many European countries, there was still a dread that sooner or later this country would be targeted by those who wished only to kill and maim ordinary citizens by the planting of bombs.

In February 1894, a bomb exploded near the Royal Observatory at Greenwich. This was, to use the modern expression, an 'own goal', in which the bomber himself died. He turned out to be a French anarchist. A month later, a bomb exploded outside a post office in New Cross Road in south London. Nobody was injured by the explosion, but it caused a fire which practically destroyed the building. There were other attacks on post offices in the area during the summer of 1894, before the campaign ended as abruptly as it had begun.

Then, as now, the police kept an eye on subversive groups and during a public meeting in the London district of Deptford on 24 January 1897, a plainclothes officer was intrigued to hear discussion turning to the manufacture and use of the explosive nitroglycerine. One member of the audience seemed to be very knowledgeable on this subject and talked at length about the difficulties of carrying out the process in a domestic setting. The speaker was 36-year-old Rollo Richards and a warrant was obtained to search his home. When the police raided Richards' home, they discovered that it was a bomb factory and there was evidence to suggest that it had been he who had been behind the bombings of the post offices in 1894. He was arrested and charged with, 'Feloniously causing an explosion by gunpowder, likely to endanger life'. When Richards appeared at the Central Criminal Court, better known as the Old Bailey, on 5 April 1897, there was some sympathy for him. He had in the past spent time in a lunatic asylum and the general view seemed to be that he had been used as a pawn by those more deeply involved in Anarchist politics. Rather than the sentence of life imprisonment which most convicted bombers had received up to that time, Richards was sent to prison for only seven years.

At ten past seven on the evening of Monday 26 April 1897, just three weeks after Rollo Richards had been sent to prison, a Metropolitan Railway train pulled into Aldersgate Station; now renamed Barbican. It was a workmen's commuter train, packed with men and women returning home after a day's work. One of the passengers was Harry Pitts, a 35-year-old manual worker, originally from Devon but now living in the working-class suburb of Tottenham. Almost as soon as the train had come to a halt, there was a deafening explosion and one of the carriages, carriage No. 93, was split in two by the blast. The glass canopy above the platform was shattered, sending shards of broken glass raining down on those standing on the platform. Another train had many of its windows blown out by the force of the blast. A lot of injuries were caused by flying glass, but Harry Pitts, who had been standing nearest to the spot where the explosion had occurred, was gravely injured and died later that day at St Bartholomew's Hospital. A contemporary drawing of this incident may be seen in Illustration 16.

At first, it was thought that a leaking gas pipe might have caused the explosion, but when Colonel Majendie, the Chief Government Inspector of Explosives visited the station and examined carriage No. 93, which had been the seat of the explosion, he soon found that the blast had come from inside the train, rather than from beneath. Not only that, but he discovered traces of dynamite in the shattered carriage; proof that a bomb had been planted on the train.

No clue was ever uncovered which might indicate who was responsible for the Aldersgate bombing. In view of the fact that the explosion occurred only a few weeks after the jailing of an anarchist bomber, it seemed a reasonable assumption that friends of Rollo Richards had been behind the attack, although the police also investigated the idea that Irish nationalists had been to blame. The inquest on Harry Pitts took place four days after his death and brought in a verdict of 'wilful murder by person or persons unknown'.

A bizarre memento of the bombing of the Tube train in 1897 may be seen at the London Transport Museum in Covent Garden. Part of the carriage destroyed by the explosion was fashioned into a miniature replica of the side of carriage No. 93 and even painted in the livery of the Metropolitan Railway. This strange item was then incorporated into an inkwell, which was for some years used by an official of the line.

Lynching, the summary execution by vigilantes of a supposed criminal, is the sort of thing one associates more with the Wild West than with commuting! Nevertheless, one of the last cases of lynching in British history actually involved commuters. The two murders at which we have so far looked were committed against commuters, one working class and the other belonging to the upper middle class. Commuters have not only been the victims of murder though. On one notable occasion, a group of angry commuters banded together on the spur of the moment and carried out a murder, one for which nobody was ever brought to justice. This incident, which took place in the Scottish city of

Glasgow in 1922, must rank as one of the most peculiar incidents in the history of commuting.

We have seen in previous chapters how different types of public transport became more or less the exclusive domain of different social groups. Buses, in Victorian London, were very much the preserve of the middle classes, whereas trams, from their very beginning, were used chiefly by working-class people. These trends were quite inflexible for decades and the wrong person using a type of public transport which was not associated with his class or social standing could expect disapproval and resentment. No City clerk would expect to find himself sitting next to a labourer on the morning bus to the office and nor would the working men on cheap trams in the late evening expect to find a well-dressed citizen sharing their own favourite means of transport. Such a passenger might provoke raised eyebrows, because there was a territorial feel about trams, which working people used both to commute to work and also for their leisure activities.

In Glasgow in the years following the end of the First World War, this class-based division of public transport was particularly noticeable. On 11 September 1922, a ship docked in the Clyde and the ship's cook then travelled from there to his home in Glasgow. Robert Alexander Stewart was 35 and, when he was not at sea, shared a house in the Ibrox district of Glasgow with his wife and also a widowed friend of his. This friend's wife had died in childbirth and his five-year-old son lived with Stewart's sister-in-law, in another part of Glasgow. Stewart was very fond of the little boy and as soon as he got home, he set off to bring the boy home to stay with him while he was ashore.

Stewart's sister-in-law lived in the Cumbuslang area of Glasgow and when he arrived there, in the evening, he met the child and then took him onto a tram heading back to Ibrox. Robert Stewart was dressed smartly, in a suit, and the child with him looked shabby in comparison and was not wearing any shoes. The sight of this well-dressed man, accompanied by a ragged-looking child was enough to anger some of the passengers on the tram, who were in the main working people heading home after a day's work. The previous year, there had been several cases in Scotland of children being abducted and abused and two women on the tram were suspicious of Robert Stewart, firstly because he was a single man in the company of a child, but chiefly because of the apparent disparity in class between him and the child who was with him. John Buchanan, the conductor of the tram, said later that some passengers had told him that the man with the child was of a 'different type' from the boy, by which he understood that the child was working class, but the man appeared not to be. There is no doubt at all that class played a major role on what happened next. One woman, deciding that this smart-looking stranger was trying to take advantage of a working-class boy from their own neighbourhood, pulled Alastair Sinclair away from the man he knew as 'Uncle Bob'. When Stewart protested, the cry was raised that he was a kidnapper.

There must have been a nightmarish air about the situation for the ship's cook, who was simply taking the little boy home to his father. Other passengers became involved and took the little boy further away from the man he was with and there began a furious and chaotic scene. In effect, Robert Stewart was driven from the tram and it appeared to the conductor that he was fleeing. The man then blew a police whistle and some of those on the tram chased after the hapless man whom they had now decided was a child molester. In the street, a hue and cry was raised and Stewart was set upon by a mob. A number of people began kicking and punching him and by the time police officer appeared on the scene, the ship's cook was severely injured. He died later that day in the infirmary. A post mortem examination showed that Robert Alexander Stewart had twelve severe external wounds and five broken bones. In plain terms, he had been beaten to death by the infuriated commuters from the tram. Two men, James Stevenson and Robert Caskie, were eventually arrested and charged with murder as a result of the lynching. When they appeared at the High Court on 29 December 1922, before Lord Alness, charged with the murder of Robert Stewart; they both pleaded 'Not Guilty'. The evidence against Stevenson and Caskie was not particularly strong and the jury took just fifteen minutes to return a verdict of 'Not Proven'. This verdict, unique to Scotland, means that there is great suspicion, but not enough evidence to convict the defendants.

We have in this chapter looked at three murders; all of which were significant in one way or another from the perspective of commuting. The first was that of Thomas Briggs, who was the first person to be murdered on a railway train, the second that of the first death resulting from a terrorist attack on a tube train and the third that of a man murdered by an enraged mob of commuters. It is time now to look at one of the most mysterious disasters ever to befall British commuters; a shocking incident which some believe to be the worst instance of mass murder ever committed in the United Kingdom. If so, this one act would eclipse anything seen during the conflict in Northern Ireland and would be among the greatest number of victims which any murderer has ever claimed at one go. Forty-two people died in the event at which we shall now look; all of them London commuters.

At four o'clock in the morning on 28 February 1975, Tube driver Leslie Newson got up, had breakfast and shaved. Before leaving the South London block of flats where he lived, he went back to the bedroom and kissed his wife on the forehead, as he did every morning before he went off to work. That day, he was planning to buy a car for his daughter and had with him £270 in cash. Newson was driving Tube trains between West Drayton, a station near Heathrow Airport, and Moorgate. Moorgate is the end of the line for that particular stretch of line, terminating in a blind tunnel, at the end of which is a five-foot thick concrete wall.

None of the men with whom Leslie Newson came into contact that morning noticed anything in the least unusual about him. After he had completed one trip from West Drayton to Moorgate and back, he had a tea break along with a few other drivers and guards in a signal box. One of the other men asked if Newson could let him have a few spoonfuls of sugar for his tea, as he had run out. Leslie Newson handed over his own sugar, saying to the man, 'Go easy with it, I shall want another cup when I come off duty.'

Among the other drivers, Newson had the reputation for being a very cautious and reliable man. He tended to slow down more when he entered a station than other drivers and always brought his train to a smooth and gentle halt. He was famous for being a man who didn't like to take risks. On his fourth journey that morning, Newson took the train from West Drayton at precisely 8:39 am and set off on the three-mile trip to Moorgate. The journey was uneventful, with the careful driver behaving in his usual careful way. By the time that the train was approaching the final stop at Moorgate, the front three coaches were packed with commuters. These coaches were crowded because they were the ones nearest to the exit from the platform at Moorgate and, being commuters, every second counted when racing from the train to leave the station and get to their offices.

It was not until the Tube train which Leslie Newson was driving actually emerged from the tunnel and entered the station at Moorgate that anybody noticed anything in the least unusual. In stark contrast to his usual caution, rather than having slowed down to a crawl, the train which Newson was driving had accelerated; in the words of one member of London Underground staff on the platform at the time, 'It burst from the tunnel like an express train'. It must be borne in mind that this was the end of the line and that the train was now heading at full speed towards a solid concrete wall. There was a maximum speed of 15 miles per hour for trains entering the station at Moorgate, but Leslie Newson seldom reached even that speed, preferring to approach the platform at five or ten miles an hour.

There were several eyewitnesses to what happened next and their testimony makes fascinating reading. All are agreed that Newson was sitting upright, with his eyes open and no expression of fear on his face. He looked just as he normally did upon bringing his train into a station. He must have continued to grip the controls which were causing the train to move forward at full speed, for if he had fainted or relaxed his grip for any reason at all, then the so-called 'dead man's handle' would have brought the train to a halt. In fact two remarkable things were noted about Newson, when his body was later recovered from the wreckage of the cab. One was that his hand was still firmly on the controls and the second that before the impact, which he must surely have been anticipating, he made no attempt to throw up either of his hands instinctively to protect his face. He had simply carried on driving into the 60-foot tunnel which extended beyond the end of the platform, and then straight into a concrete wall. The first three coaches concertinaed into each other, the third rising up and ploughing over the roof of the second. The space between the floor and the roof of one of these carriages was reduced to a mere two feet. Following the crash of the impact and the screech of metal, there was a moment's silence. Then the signalman called London Transport and alerted them to what was beginning to look like a catastrophe.

It is often only in the event of a disaster that the discovery is made that emergency services are woefully lacking some vital piece of equipment. So it proved on this occasion, because when the fire brigade and medical teams arrived on the scene, one of the first priorities was establishing a link between those working on the wreckage of the train and others on the surface. A field telephone system was at first tried, of a vintage which might have been more appropriate to a Second World War battlefield, but the cables could not stretch all the way to the surface. This meant that messages had to be conveyed by word of mouth and passed from one person to another amid the clatter and din of the machinery being used to free the trapped victims. This turned into a grotesque and deadly version of the party game 'Chinese Whispers'. A doctor was in urgent need of the painkiller Entonox, a gaseous mixture of nitrous oxide and oxygen. His request for a cylinder to be sent down from the surface, began as, 'The doctor needs Entonox'. By the time it reached those coordinating the rescue mission on ground level, it had become, 'The doctor needs an empty box'!

The scene which met the rescuers was unbelievably gruesome. Apart from the obviously mangled corpses were the bodies of those who had simply died of internal trauma. In one carriage, a row of commuting businessmen sat patiently in their seats, their briefcases on their laps. All were dead, but with open, staring eyes. This was so unnerving that firemen covered them with a sheet as they worked. By the evening, all but two of the survivors had been removed from the crash site. A young woman called Margaret Liles was inextricably trapped by her left foot. In the end, an amputation had to be carried out in order to free her. Then the job could begin in earnest of taking the forty-three dead bodies of those who had died in the crash up to the surface.

Even before the rescue operation had been completed, there was speculation about the cause of this, the worst Tube train disaster of all time. From the start, attention was focused upon Leslie Newson, who had so inexplicably driven his train full of commuters into a concrete wall at 40 miles per hour. Since it was known that Newson had been conscious and in control of the train right up to the very moment of impact, there could really be only three possibilities. One hypothesis was that Newson had suffered from a momentary lapse of concentration, perhaps being preoccupied with personal matters such as the car which he was due to but later that day. This was unlikely: Newson was a famously cautious and careful driver. There remained either a medical condition which suddenly afflicted the driver as he entered Moorgate, or the shocking notion that he might have committed suicide, taking with him over forty strangers in the process. Efforts to discover what had caused Leslie Newson to behave as he did were hampered by the decomposition of his body. One theory was that he had suffered a very minor stroke, which might have had the effect of paralysing him. Unfortunately, there was no evidence for this idea and Newson's brain was, by the time that his body was recovered, not in a fit state to be carefully examined.

If the Moorgate crash had been caused by the suicide of Leslie Newson, then he would have been as guilty of the murder of the forty-two passengers who died as were the 7/7 suicide bombers. One clue was that alcohol was found in the driver's bloodstream and also in the milk which he had used that day for his tea. It was later suggested that its presence could have been explained by natural fermentation, which can produce alcohol. The only difficulty with this idea is that the blood of other victims of the crash did not test positive in this way. In the absence of any other evidence, the only facts that we know are that Leslie Newson drove a train full of commuters at full speed into a five-foot thick concrete wall. His eyes were open and he was apparently conscious and awake as he did so and he made no attempt to operate the brakes. It was, to all external appearances, a deliberate act. One theory was that Newson had decided to commit suicide that morning and then taken a stiff alcoholic drink in his tea to give him Dutch courage to go through with the plan.

The truth is, we shall never know just what it was that impelled a reliable and conscientious driver to plough into a blind tunnel as Leslie Newson did that February morning in 1975. Suicide and multiple murder is probably a better explanation than most, but in the absence of further evidence, we can only guess. The inquest brought in a verdict of accidental death, but this was perhaps an act of kindness towards the Leslie Newson's family. To brand a dead man a suicide and mass murderer would have been a dreadful and pointless thing to do and would not have done anybody any good.

No account of the violent deaths of commuters would be complete without mention of the suicide attacks which were launched against the London Underground in 2005. On Wednesday 6 July 2005, the announcement was made that the 2012 Olympic Games would be held in London. There was huge excitement at the news, with Londoners feeling that their city was now the centre of world attention. So it was, but within twenty-four hours, this attention was to be magnified a hundred-fold, in a way that nobody could possibly have imagined.

The morning rush hour in London reaches its peak at about 9:00 am, when the Tubes, buses and suburban trains are all disgorging their hundreds of thousands of commuters onto the streets of the capital. At 8:49 am on Thursday 7 July 2005, there was a loud bang in the tunnel linking Liverpool Street Station with Aldgate. This tunnel carries both Circle Line trains and also those of the Hammersmith and City lines. Shortly afterwards, there was an explosion on a tube train which had just left Edgware, heading towards Paddington. A third explosion took place on a Piccadilly Line train between King's Cross and Russell Square. All three explosions took place in the space of less than a minute.

At first, there was a great deal of confusion about what had happened. Because reports came through from stations at either end of the tunnels, it was thought to begin with that there had actually been six, rather than three explosions. It took some little while for the true nature of the events to be understood. London Transport assumed at first that a power surge had caused the bangs and there were also rumours that a train had been derailed. Gradually, it became clear that something far worse than electrical faults were to blame. By the time that it was dawning on everybody that what had happened was the almost inconceivable, the simultaneous detonation of three terrorist bombs, another explosion took place, this time on a bus in Tavistock Square.

The effects of the four bombs which exploded that morning were very different and were ultimately dependent upon the different methods for constructing underground railway lines at which we looked in an earlier chapter. The first two took place on the Circle Line, whose tunnels were constructed by using the cut-and-cover method. This makes for wide tunnels, with plenty of room all around. The Piccadilly Line though is a true 'tube', being driven deep underground with narrow tunnels leaving only inches of clearance between the walls of the carriages and the walls of the tunnels. It will be recalled that when Irish terrorists set off bombs on the Underground in 1883 and 1885, these were in cut-and-cover tunnels. Nobody was killed in these attacks. The force of the blasts were able to dissipate easily in the roomy tunnels. This was not at all the case with the bomb which exploded deep beneath the earth on the Piccadilly Line train on 7 July 2005. There, rather than being free to escape, the expanding gases of the explosion were reflected by the tunnel walls back into the carriage, where they caused carnage. In the carriage on the Piccadilly Line train, twenty-six men and women were killed, twice as many as in the other two explosions put together.

The attacks, which were the first suicide bombings ever seen in Britain, were carried out by fanatical Islamists, apparently intending to protest against the invasions of Iraq and Afghanistan by British and American forces. In effect, they were a blow against the Christian West in revenge for the supposed sufferings of Muslims in the Third World. It had presumably escaped the notice of those carrying out the atrocities that London is one of the most multicultural cities in the world and that its commuters are drawn from the widest possible spectrum. A glance at the casualty lists for the bombings makes this very plain; it must be vanishingly improbably that somebody called Shahara Islam would be a supporter of British policy in the Middle East! Among those killed were Indians, Jews, Africans and members of a dozen various nationalities; Atique Sharifi, Shayanuja Parathasangary, Ojara Ikeagwu, Gamze Gunoral, Ihab Slimane and Behnaz Mozakka all being victims of the atrocities.

Apart from the four bombers who died, fifty-two innocent people, most of them commuters, were killed in what became known as the 7/7 bombings. Precisely two weeks later, on Thursday 21 July, attempts were made to cause another massacre. Three men on Underground trains and one on a bus tried to set off identical bombs to those used in the earlier attacks. These consisted of backpacks filled with large quantities of a homemade explosive which had been produced from hydrogen peroxide. Producing explosives of this sort though, which can be undertaken in a domestic bathtub, is a tricky business. The combination of substances used can sometimes explode prematurely, while the chemical process is taking place or, more commonly still, the result will be an inert and harmless compound. This is what happened, mercifully, during the 21 July attacks. The four would-be bombers tried to set off their bombs, but although the detonators exploded; the main charges did not.

The advent of the suicide bomber on the London Underground produced for a time the curious custom of 'carriage hopping', in which commuters who did not care for the look of some dark-skinned fellow passenger with bulky luggage would jump off the train at the next station, sometimes to move to another carriage and at other times to wait for a different train entirely. For a period over the summer of 2005, it was feared that every other morning Tube train might be carrying dedicated and suicidal terrorists, whose only aim in life was to slaughter as many London commuters as they possibly could. There can be no doubt that mass murder was committed against commuters on the London Underground in 2005. Less certain, although quite probable, is the idea that a serial killer was for three decades or so preying upon those travelling by Tube.

During the 1950s and 1960s there circulated among commuters using the London Underground something in the nature of an urban myth, to the effect that there was a murderer who pushed random men and women in front of approaching tube trains. Some claimed to have heard of such cases, others were sufficiently cautious never to stand at the edge of the platform, just to be on the safe side. Seasoned commuters would sometimes stand back a little and brace themselves as a train approached; just in case somebody standing behind gave them a shove which might propel them onto the tracks. It was just one of those stories which crop up from time to time in any environment and there was no real reason to think that there was anything in it. Until 1983, that is. That was the year that an Irish vagrant by the name of Kiernan Kelly was arrested for attempted murder, having allegedly pushed an elderly man onto the tracks in front of a Tube train at Kensington Station.

In 1953, 25-year-old Kiernan Kelly had arrived in London, having left Ireland to seek his fortune. He was a covert homosexual and, after a friend asked him if he was married, got it into his head that his secret was about to come out. After brooding about this for some time, he later claimed that he had pushed the friend under a Tube train at Tooting Bec Station. He was, not surprisingly, unable to forget this act and turned to drink to obliterate the memory. Perhaps as a result of this, over the years Kelly drifted into a life of alcoholism, eventually becoming a tramp. He spent time prison, chiefly for offences involving dishonesty and drunken fights. From time to time, there was the suspicion that Kelly might have been mixed up with crimes a good deal worse than picking pockets and falling down drunk in the street. On 25 December 1975, the corpse of another vagrant called Hector Fisher was found in the graveyard of a church at Clapham, in south London. He had been beaten to death. The police found a number of people who had been seen drinking with Fisher a few hours before his death and interviews them all. No arrests were made. One of those to whom they spoke was Kiernan Kelly.

Eighteen months after Hector Fisher's murder, an elderly tramp was found dead in Soho. The man, 68-year-old Maurice Weighly, had been savagely assaulted. His face and genitals had been mutilated and a broken bottle had been forced into his rectum. Two tramps were apprehended with bloodstains on their clothing and one of them claimed that the other had committed the murder. The man he accused was Kiernan Kelly. Kelly was brought to trial, but his defence lawyer was able to show that the only witness against him had been extremely drunk at the time and was a chronic alcoholic. Kelly was acquitted. The man who had testified against Kiernan Kelly vanished after the trial and was never seen again.

It was the belief of the police that Kelly was a dangerous individual, but there was no way of keeping track of a rough–sleeping alcoholic and so there was little to be done. They had no further dealings with Kiernan Kelly until May 1983, when he was seen by several witnesses to push a man under an approaching Tube train at Kensington Station. This time, there seemed to be no way out for Kelly, as he was arrested and charged with attempted murder.

Almost unbelievably, when the trial of Kiernan Kelly for attempted murder took place, the jury found themselves unable to agree and Kelly was turned loose once more. Shortly after his release, another man was pushed to his death under a train at Oval Station. On 4 August 1983, Kelly was arrested once more, this time for being drunk and disorderly and also for a robbery. He was locked in a cell for the night with another drunk called William Boyd. Boyd's snoring annoyed Kelly and so he beat him almost to death, fracturing his skull in the process, and then strangled him.

It was at this point that Kiernan Kelly made a number of confessions, some involving the murder of fellow tramps and others about a series of murders which he claimed to have committed on the London Underground. He confessed to Hector Fisher's murder, eight years earlier, with which he was charged. In 1984, Kelly was sentenced to life imprisonment, for both the manslaughter of William Boyd and the murder of Hector Fisher. No action was taken about the fifteen or so other men he claimed to have murdered by pushing them under Tube trains.

In 2015, a book was published which suggested that it was suspected that a serial killer had been at work on the Northern Line, but that acting under instructions from the Home Office, this had not been publicised, for fear of causing panic among those who used the Tube regularly. It is hard to know what to make of all this. Some of the murders which Kelly claimed to have committed had already been recorded as accidents or suicides. There can be no doubt that he did seem to have knowledge of a number of deaths on the Underground system and had possibly been present at the time that the men met their deaths. Beyond that, it is impossible to go.

The idea of a homicidal maniac stalking the London Underground, surreptitiously shoving unsuspecting passengers in front of approaching trains is calculated to strike at the deepest anxieties of the average commuter and it is highly likely that had it been known during the 1960s that such a killer was operating in the capital, then there would indeed have been panic.

Chapter 10

Metroland and Becontree: A Third of the British Population become Commuters

F rom the Industrial Revolution, the growth of commuting in Britain was steady. At various times, there were sudden surges in the numbers of those commuting to work. This happened, for example, with the introduction of buses and then of trams. In general, though, the increase in numbers was not dramatic. This changed suddenly in the twenty years between the end of the First World War in 1918 and the beginning of the Second World War in 1939. During this twenty-year period, something in the region of a third of the British population became commuters. Part of this was the unplanned development of new urban areas on the fringes of cities, but the majority of new commuters were created quite deliberately by the social policies of various local authorities. Over the course of those few years, 30 per cent of the people in this country were moved from their homes in the centres of cities and rehoused in the suburbs and countryside. It was the greatest movement of population ever seen in the country, before or since.

As the twentieth century drew on, commuters benefited from the symbiotic relationship which increasingly existed between railway companies and builders. It is a debatable point, which of the two types of business did best out commuters. In the early years of the railways, there was no realisation at all that there might be money to be made from catering for commuters living in the suburbs of British cities. Initially, those building and running the railways worked on the assumption that very few passengers would be using their trains on a regular basis and that most journeys would be from one city to another, rather than over short distances or even just travelling from one part of a city to another. Lines running from the centres of cities typically had no halts for eight or ten miles until they were well clear of the edge of the city. The notion that anybody might wish to catch a train from the suburbs simply did not occur to anybody.

By the turn of the century, however, it was obvious that builders were seeing great opportunities in throwing up housing alongside tram routes and railway lines. That this would in turn generate custom for the transport systems soon became apparent, as many of those who came to live in the new developments were to be commuters. These men and women would be buying tickets twice a day to use the trains and trams to go to work. To see how this relationships between transport links and property developers worked, we shall look again at the London suburb of Ilford.

In 1839, the newly-founded Great Eastern Railway Company laid a line from the East End out into Essex, to the little market town of Romford, 15 miles away. There were only two intermediate stops, one at Stratford and the other at Ilford. Other than those two halts, the train ran straight through the countryside, past little villages and hamlets. Nobody thought for a moment that the residents of such places might wish to board a train and if they did, then they would be expected to make their way five miles or so to either Ilford or Stratford.

Towards the end of the nineteenth century, when the railway from London to Romford had been going for something over a half a century, a property developer called Cameron Corbett decided that the land beyond Ilford, in the open fields of Seven Kings, was perfect for building a new community of commuters. He bought up vast tracts of land and then laid out streets of comfortable houses of the kind which might appeal to managers, businessmen and clerks. The only difficulty was, of course, that there was no convenient way for these people to get to their jobs; most of which were likely to be in central London. Few of them would be keen on a two-mile walk to the station every morning. Corbett approached the Great Eastern and persuaded them that it would be profitable for them to build two new stations to serve the commuters who would soon be moving into the new town which he was busily engaged in erecting. In this case, it was the building of commuter housing which prompted the railway stations; in other cases, the reverse happened.

To see how commuting was growing during the twentieth century, we might find it instructive to look at two projects which were both conceived and executed with the sole, immediate and direct intention of producing new commuters who would live in the Home Counties, travelling in and out of London each day to work. Counterparts of these two schemes are to be found in all Britain's large cities and the reason for choosing two near London is simply that Metro-land and Becontree are almost mirror-images of each other which perfectly illustrate the trends in commuting during the years before the Second World War.

Most people have heard vaguely of Metro-land, even if it is only from having seen or read about John Betjeman's documentary of that title, which was first shown on television in 1973. Betjeman was Poet Laureate when the programme was made and his commentary was partly in verse. *Metro-land* was a hymn to the suburbs of North West London which are served by the Metropolitan Line. Of course, John Betjeman did not coin the expression Metro-land; that had already been in common usage for over fifty years when the television programme of the same name was broadcast. When Evelyn Waugh wished to give a character in his 1928 novel *Decline and Fall* an amusingly topical name, he chose Viscount Metroland.

Metro-land had been devised when the Metropolitan Railway was extending its line North West; out of London and into the counties of Hertfordshire and Buckinghamshire. When this process was begun during the First World War, the company published a booklet called, rather unimaginatively, *Guide to the Extension Line*. A far catchier title was soon found and it became the *Metro-land Guide*. According to this publication, Metro-land was, 'a country with elastic borders that each visitor can draw for himself'. What the inhabitants of this mythical land all had in common was of course that they were to be commuters. The purpose of all these lyrical accounts about an imaginary kingdom, was nothing more than to sell people houses which had been built on land belonging to the Metropolitan Railway. Metro-land was to be a land full of commuters who were compelled to use the railway each day to get to their jobs. A poster advertising the delights of Metro-land may be seen in Illustration 17. A map produced by the Metropolitan Railway at the height of its promotion of Metro-land, shows that the railway line stretches north and west of Baker Street through Neasden, into Amersham and then up to Stoke Mandeville, ending at Verney Junction. Incredibly, the Metropolitan Line in those days reached fifty miles from central London.

Before returning to the subject of Metro-land, with particular reference to the architecture of the 'country', we must look at another commuters' paradise which was being promoted at the same time as Metro-land, although for a very different kind of commuter. If we can be reasonably sure that most readers will have heard of Metro-land and have some idea, however indistinct about where and what it was, we may be equally confident that not one person in a thousand is likely to know anything at all about Becontree, which was being developed at the same time that the joys of Metro-land were being widely extolled.

Becontree and Metro-land are like two sides of the same coin, in that both were intended to cater for commuters who had moved into the suburbs and the Home Counties and would be using public transport each day to get to work. There, the similarities begin and end. The purpose of creating Metro-land and marketing the idea was to lure middle-class commuters into buying houses on the outskirts of London and further out. This would benefit the Metropolitan Railway both by ensuring that these house buyers would, perforce, become regular users of the railway line into Town and also of course because the houses themselves had been built on land owned by the railway. This was private enterprise generating a new type of commuter. Becontree, on the other hand, was the brainchild of a local authority: the London County Council. The commuters whom they were producing would be working-class slum dwellers from the inner city, families who would, to use the modern jargon of local authority housing departments, be 'decanted' from crowded streets and tenement buildings, and then moved to a newly-built township in the Essex marshes. Like those who bought homes in Metro-land, those moving to Becontree would, it was assumed, be commuting to London, there being no industry or other opportunities for work in the vast new estate to which they were moving.

The creation of Becontree was part of the greatest movement of people in the history of Britain and it took place between the two world wars. In the course of that time, almost a third of the population of Britain was transferred from the central parts of cities to their outskirts. The effect was to create a nation of working-class commuters, to complement the middle-class ones who were becoming the residents of Metro-land and similar developments. The fact that this great migration has been all but forgotten today is curious. Between 1919 and 1939, a period of less than twenty years, twelve million people in this country were moved to new homes. It was a transmigration on the scale of Stalin's Russia and yet nobody objected: indeed, this far-sighted act of social engineering was universally applauded. As the Minister of Health Sir Kingsley Wood said just before the outbreak of the Second World War, 'Removals on so large a scale involving so high a proportion of the population have never taken place before in the whole course of our history.'

The aim of this mass movement was to transfer those living in the crowded slums of Britain's inner cities to the suburbs and countryside. Because only houses and flats were being built for them and not factories or other places to work; the expectation from the beginning was that these people would become commuters. Over 20 per cent of Birmingham's entire population were moved into new local authority housing built on the countryside around the city. The same thing happened in Glasgow and also in Manchester. Over a million council houses were built between the wars, the vast majority of them on the fields and farmland just outside the boundaries of the cities. The new housing estates were generous in scale and gave working-class families the sort of space which, until that time, had only been available to middle-class people living in the suburbs. In the centre of London and Birmingham, many people were still living in the cramped streets which had been thrown up in a hurry during the Industrial Revolution. The average density was seventy houses to an acre.

Local authorities were now budgeting for a mere twelve houses for each acre. The difference in the environments was astonishing.

The effect of both Becontree and Metro-land, and similar schemes being undertaken in provincial cities, was to draw Londoners out further from the centre of their city, the working classes from the slums which were still such a notable and undesirable feature of the inner city and the middle classes from the suburbs, many of which had become less attractive through the 'wrong' sort of residents moving there. Metro-land promised that middle-class commuters could live in their own miniature country estate, in a Tudor-style manor house surrounded by its own little grounds. This was an attractive proposition indeed for bank managers and shopkeepers, that they might live in the style of Elizabethan landowners, rather than being stuck in drab and featureless city streets of identical houses. It was to be a step change from the suburban life of commuters like the Pooters, who had to make do with Holloway. The promise for the working-class families who were to be lured to Becontree was a little different. Most of those who moved there were grateful for the offer of a bathroom and an indoor lavatory. They came either from the crowded tenement buildings, like the Peabody Estates around King's Cross or from the rows of two-up and two-down terraced houses of Whitechapel and Mile End. For such people, anything was likely to be an improvement in their living conditions.

The differing ambitions of the two groups of people leaving London for the rural areas of Essex, Hertfordshire and Buckinghamshire are intimately bound up with that that archetypal home of the British commuter; the three-bedroom semi-detached house. If there is one type of dwelling which came over the years to sum up and symbolise the commuter lifestyle, it was this. The three-bedroom semi was to be the shorthand sign for all things suburban and relating to commuters, mocked and despised by the younger generation of baby-boomers as symbolising all that they rejected about the lifestyle of their parents. For those who moved to Metro-land, the chances were that their semi-detached house would be in the style popularly known as mock-Tudor. A look at the origins of the mock-Tudor semi-detached home will shed a little light on both suburban commuters in general and the situation in developments like Becontree and Metro-land.

The mock-Tudor style, more correctly known as Tudor Revival, was part of the Arts and Crafts movement of Victorian Britain. It was meant as a counter to the Gothic and Neo-Georgian styles which were so popular in the nineteenth century, harking back to the Elizabethan Age of domestic tranquillity and rural charm. The aim was to produce buildings which looked rather like sixteenth-century manor houses or cottages, with wood beams showing against white plastered walls, instead of brickwork. Of course, from the very beginning, a degree of deception and artifice was needed in order to reproduce the architectural style of that era. The exposed dark wooden beams that we see on genuine Elizabethan houses are actually supporting structures: they are necessary to hold up the building. Typically, the framework of the building would be wooden and the walls made of lathe and plaster. Their distinctive visual appearance was no more than a by-product of the methods and material used to build them. In Tudor Revival, such external features are typically a sham. The structure itself is built from bricks, like any normal house. Then a plaster coat is applied to the outside and planks fixed to the exterior walls. This results in a crude pastiche of a sixteenth-century building, artificially manufactured for purely aesthetic reasons. Two mock-Tudor semi-detached houses of this period may be seen in Illustrations 18 and 19.

One quite understands Victorian craftsmen like William Morris being keen on recreating an earlier and supposedly gentler and more artistic age, but why on Earth should middle-class commuters have been so taken with this architectural style that mock-Tudor should have come to symbolise their entire lifestyle? There are two reasons. One motive of the sort of people who moved out to Metro-land and other fashionable districts outside other British cities had for embracing the Tudor Revival style of house was pure snobbery. The tenement blocks of inner cities were, in the main, built to look like large terraces of Georgian townhouses. A typical Peabody Estate would consist of tall redbrick structures with various little architectural flourishes such as round false windows high up on one side. These suggested the kind of thing which one might find below the eaves of an eighteenth-century mansion. The terraced streets in poorer districts also had often a faintly Georgian air about them, being blocky and rectangular, with no attempt made to conceal the fact that they were made entirely of brick. The Tudor Revival home was in stark contrast to the appearance of working-class housing. It was predominantly black and white, rather than reddish-brown. The roofs were higher and with a steeper pitch, and red tiles, instead of grey slates; leaded lights or stained glass, rather than plain casements. In short, the houses of this style were to look as little like the homes of working-class people as possible. One consequence of this snobbish attitude to architectural style was that the mock-Tudor semi became the ultimate aim of many working-class people. Anybody living in such a house had definitely 'made it' and escaped from their proletarian roots.

There was another reason for the desirability of the mock-Tudor house among the better-off type of commuter and to understand this, we need to consider once more the poster at which we looked in the Introduction. It will be recalled that this was actually an advertisement for Metro-land and aimed to persuade people to move to Edgware and leave behind the bleak streets of terraced housing which they might currently be living. Inevitably, the cottages shown in the delightful country scene which showed Edgware, were black-and-white Tudor buildings. This was what Tudor architecture suggested; a rural idyll, far away from the city. The quotation from Abraham Cowley also sheds light on the psychology of the appeal: 'I never had any other desire so strong and so like to covetousness as that one which I have had always, that I might be Master of a small House and a Large garden, with moderate conveniences joined to them.' A small house and a large garden just about sums up what many middle-class commuters yearned for. This combination enabled even the humblest clerk to emulate the landed gentry of a bygone age, albeit on a modest scale. A three-bedroom semi tricked out to look like an Elizabethan manor house, surrounded by its own grounds. The image is very much that of Wemmick's 'castle' in Walworth, in which a man might fancy himself lord of all that he surveyed. No matter how harried and put upon he might be at the office, when such a homeowner returned in the evening he was master of his own estate. The white plastered walls and dark beams on the front of the house helped maintain this illusion. It will also be recalled that when the suburbs around Ilford in Essex were being built, there was a definite and strong tendency to avoid using either 'street' or 'road' in the addresses; 'lane', 'avenue', 'gardens' or 'park' being preferred. This was to suggest a rural location, rather than a built-up area. The mock-Tudor semi was part of the same pretence, that the commuters living in a house tricked out to resemble a sixteenth-century cottage in such-and-such 'avenue' were living not on the fringes of a city, but actually in the countryside.

The estates built by the Metropolitan Railway were intended to echo and reinforce this idea of country living. They were given names like the Cedars Estate, Grange and Kingsbury. No suggestion that any of these areas of mock-Tudor housing were just round the corner from Neasden. The illusion was artfully constructed: a crude copy of a Tudor cottage on an estate named Kingsbury and the owner was able to persuade himself that he was the next best thing to a country squire!

In time, of course, the three-bedroom semi-detached house became the most sought after type of residence across the whole of Britain. It was not just those moving to Metro-land who wanted a mock-Tudor semi; it became the gold standard against which all property was measured. This is still the case today. A survey of estate agents in the summer of 2014 showed that this type of property was more sought-after than any other. Part of this might of course be simply because there are more of them about than any other kind of house or flat: they make up a third of England's housing stock.

In Becontree, semi-detached houses were not so common. Instead, there were rows and rows of terraced homes. Nor were the houses being built there, between the Essex towns of Ilford and Dagenham, disguised as a sixteenth-century cottages either: they were just constructed of ordinary unadorned bricks. Uniformity was the key to this vast new town, which covered four square miles. There was no industry, few shops and no jobs in this housing estate. It was assumed that those re-housed here would carry on working at the London docks and factories where they had been employed before moving. At first a new tramline was planned, which would run north from Becontree and link up with the Ilford Borough tramways which ran up to nearby Chadwell Heath. Nothing came of this scheme, however. By the time that the first 26,000 houses of Becontree had been completed in the mid-1930s, trams were on the point of being replaced by trolleybuses and it would have been quixotic to start laying a new line. There were, in any case, railway services running into both Fenchurch Street and Liverpool Street for these new commuters, as well as the trams running from Chadwell Heath and the various bus routes leading to London.

For those who moved into Metro-land, transport links were a little less haphazard and unplanned. The fact was that the Metropolitan Railway owned the land upon which their homes had been built and the very act of relocating to Metro-land meant that one would be using the Metropolitan Railway to get to work and back. What many of those moving to Metro-land failed to realise was that the whole enterprise was, from the very beginning, a bit of a con.

When railways were built, the Act of Parliament authorising them almost invariably stipulated that any land left over when the line had been laid must be disposed of. This had not been the case with the Acts involving the Metropolitan Railway. In the case of the Metropolitan Railway, there were specific clauses which allowed the company to retain surplus land to use for future development of the railway. From the late nineteenth century onwards, the spare land was being sold to builders. Shortly before the start of the First World War, some of the directors of the Metropolitan Railway began to wonder why they should sell the land to others to develop. Why not form a subsidiary company and reap the profits of building houses for commuters themselves? In due course, the Metropolitan Railways Country Estates Company was set up; whose directors were, almost without exception, also directors of the Metropolitan Railway. The legality of this arrangement was open to question, but it was never challenged in the courts. For the Metropolitan Railway, the setup was a huge money-spinner. They were making a good profit from selling the houses which they were busily engaged in building on their own land, safe in the knowledge that those moving into these properties would be buying season tickets for their railway as well.

The creation of so many commuters in the years between the wars was beneficial to everybody. The slums of Britain's cities were cleared and their inhabitants moved to healthier locations. The building trade flourished, which was a good thing during the Great Depression, providing work for men who might otherwise have been on the dole. For the middle classes too, there were great advantages and no real disadvantages. The mass movement of those twelve million people really laid the foundations for modern Britain, a country where, in the early twenty-first century, there have never been so many commuters. We have not yet touched, though, upon the most popular method of commuting today, which has nothing to do with the various methods of public transport at which we have so far looked. Over half the commuters in this country today get to work not by buses, trains or trams, but by that most ubiquitous means of travel, the motor car.

Chapter 11

'With Integral Garage': The Inexorable Rise of the Commuting Motorist

One method of commuting has, since the end of the Second World War, eclipsed all others, until it accounts today for around 60 per cent of all travel to and from work in the United Kingdom. The 2011 census revealed that 15.3 million people in England and Wales travel to work by driving a car or van. Another 1.4 million people are carried to work as passengers in cars and vans. The car is, without doubt, the most popular means of commuting in the country. For all their historical association with commuting, at which we have looked in previous chapters, railway trains account now only for a mere 1.4 million commuters, about 5 per cent of the total.

The triumph of the petrol engine for transporting commuters to their place of work has been a relatively recent phenomenon. The rise of commuting by car differs from the growth of public transport at which we have so far looked. Driving one's car to work is simply a reflection of what has been happening in society as a whole, rather than something like the spread of the omnibus, which was a development deliberately contrived and planned with commuters specifically in mind. The types of transport which we have examined, such as trams, tube trains and buses, were all designed with the purpose of taking people to work. This of course is why the first buses ran to the City of London and why much of the development of public transport has focused upon connecting suburbs with city centres. To see how it has come about that more people commute to work by car than all the other methods put together, we would look in vain for a pioneering architect of the trend. There is no one person like Charles Pearson, the tireless advocate of underground railways, to blame for the popularity of commuting by car. We will need instead to find out a little about the history of the motor car's ascent in general and only then try to see how it became such a major influence on the practice off commuting.

The first petrol-driven cars appeared in Europe in the 1880s, but it was to be 1894 before a British-built motor car appeared on the roads. A gas fitter and plumber called Frederick Bremer built his own car from scratch, even crafting the spark-plugs individually by hand. This strange vehicle achieved, at least according to its inventor, a speed of 20 miles per hour. Such early cars were of course curiosities and nobody in his senses would have dreamed of relying upon one of these contraptions to get to work on time in the morning!

It took some years for petrol engines to reach a level of sophistication which made them more reliable that a horse and carriage. The first motor vehicles to carry commuters were London buses and they were so notorious for breaking down that the Chief Officer of the London County Council Tramways, Aubrey Llewelyn Fell, said in 1909 that, 'Twenty years hence, motor buses will be exhibited as curios in museums'. At a time when electric trams rattled along efficiently, with few malfunctions or delays, day in and day out and carrying hundreds of thousands of commuters, this probably seemed a perfectly reasonable prediction to make. The Royal Commission on London Traffic, which had met in 1905, came to pretty much the same conclusion. They too believed that trams were likely for the foreseeable future to be of more importance than the new-fangled motor buses. In the report which they issued, the Commission said: 'We cannot recommend the postponement of tramway extension in London on the ground of any visible prospect of the supersession of tramways by motor omnibuses.'

In short, the unstoppable rise of the petrol engine was impossible to foresee in the early years of the twentieth century. At first, cars were, with few exceptions, the exclusive property of the very well-to-do. Rather than being used to take people to the office, they were more likely to be seen at Ascot or Glyndebourne. In 1907, there were just 32,000 cars on the roads of Britain. The following year though, Henry Ford began mass-producing cars, with the world's first moving assembly line and from being in the same category as the steam yacht of a millionaire, cars started to become affordable by ordinary people. By 1922 over 315,000 cars were registered in Britain.

To begin with, even mass-produced motor cars were still expensive. In 1920, a typical small car manufactured by the Austin company was selling for £495, which was equivalent to about a year's salary for a professional man. Three years later, the same company introduced the Austin Seven, which retailed for about half the price, at £225. By 1930, the cost of an Austin Seven had dropped to £125, which brought it within the reach of many more potential customers. In 1932, Ford produced their first car designed for the British market, the Model Y. Thirty-nine thousand of this model were sold in 1933, at £100 each. Motoring for the masses had arrived.

It was during the 1930s that commuting by car, private rather than public transport, began to take off in Britain. The growth of car ownership and the use of cars to get to work, either all the way or at least by taking commuters to their local railway station, caused a number of changes in Britain, the legacy of which is all around us. Until this time, urban sprawl had been associated with railway stations and tram routes. People in the suburbs usually wished to live within walking distance of the station or tram stop which would take them into town. To this extent, the development of suburbs had been planned; they were built along railway lines and tram routes. Once many people were driving cars, those building new rows of houses for commuters were not limited by the same considerations. For this reason, it was perhaps unfortunate that this explosion in car ownership happened to coincide with a nationwide agricultural slump.

When the slump hit British farming during the 1930s, many farmers were thrown into hazard financially. They had land, but planting and harvesting crops in their fields was hardly worthwhile from a strictly business point of view. Those of them with fields facing roads leading into towns and cities soon found willing buyers for their property, men who offered them a way out of their difficulties. These saviours of the small farmer were speculative builders who had cottoned on to the fact that commuters were no longer restricted in where they wished to live by the presence or absence of a railway station. Semi-detached houses, more often than not in the 'mock-Tudor' style, were thrown up along roads in areas which had previously been only open country. Many of these new houses were advertised as having 'integral garages'. It was clearly understood that the possession of a house with a garage, and by extension, ownership of a car, was a very desirable thing and likely to raise one's status considerably.

A name was soon coined for the phenomenon of building on agricultural land lining country lanes and roads; it was called 'ribbon development' and was regarded by many as a scourge. The owners of these new homes were often able either to drive to work or at least to the local station. There was a price to pay of course for all this and in this case it was a heavy one. In the five years leading up to 1934, the death toll on Britain's roads ran to 7,000 a year, the majority of them pedestrians. Some compared the terrible numbers of casualties to the figures for deaths on the battlefield during the Napoleonic Wars and found that more people were dying on the roads each year than had been killed in the course of that conflict. The author Robert Graves wrote in *The Long Weekend* that, 'Cottages near dangerous country crossroads became unofficial dressing stations', a reference to the battlefield first-aid posts of the First World War. He went on to mention that in some towns, parents began keeping their children out of school until some provision was made for their crossing the road in safety.

Significantly, the peak times for pedestrian deaths from road traffic accidents were during the rush hours of the morning and evening. Many of those 7,000 people a year being killed were victims of commuters! Some could not see what all the fuss was about. A Conservative MP, Lieutenant-Colonel Moore-Brabazon, remarked in Parliament that, 'More than 6,000 people commit suicide every year, and nobody makes a fuss about that.' Most people though felt that something would have to be done about the dreadful death toll. In 1930, the 20-mile-an-hour speed limit which had been in force for decades, and widely ignored, was abolished altogether. A Bill was later introduced that would reimpose a speed limit, this time of 30 miles per hour in built-up areas. Moore-Brabazon was vehemently opposed to any such thing. He said in a speech on 10 April 1934:

> People are getting used to the new conditions. The fact that the road is practically the great railway of the country, instead of being the playground of the young, has to be realised. No doubt many of the older Members of the House will recollect the numbers of chickens that we killed in the early days. We used to come back with the radiator stuffed with feathers. It was the same with dogs. Dogs get out of the way of motor cars nowadays, and you never kill one. There is education even in the lower animals. These things will right themselves. It may well be that we have got to the peak of road accidents, and that, even within a year or two, people will realise the extreme change that has come over our life, and that very much greater care must be taken.

As Robert Graves had observed, there were plenty of casualties from traffic accidents in the countryside, as well as the city, but it was in built-up urban areas that the effect of the car was most keenly felt, particularly during the rush hour. Having moved into a semi-detached house with a garage on a ribbon development, a few miles from the city, there was really only one way to get to work and that was by using the car for either the whole or part of the journey. It would have been seen as wilfully perverse not to do so, in an age before worries about the 'environment' and the size of one's carbon footprint were a matter of concern. As a slogan for the 1924 Scottish Motor Show put it, 'Be a motorist and have your own railway!'

One problem was of course that when only a handful of people owned cars, then they were able to slip through cities at speed, accelerating swiftly past buses or horses and carts. Now though, there were so many drivers on the roads that traffic jams and gridlocks became a routine occurrence during the rush hour. There had been difficulties with traffic causing hold-ups in the past, of course, but this was different. In Victorian Britain, the London traffic had been maddeningly slow; now, it ground completely to a halt. In 1924, a gridlock of motorised vehicles in London's Strand paralysed the area entirely for two hours. This was more than a mere traffic jam; it was the city's centre being altogether clogged up by a new means of transport. The reason for the problem was not hard to find. When buses and trams are the chief vehicles carrying people around, then each one will be holding twenty, thirty, forty or even fifty passengers. With cars, each driver is one more vehicle on the road. A tram full of passengers could translate into fifty cars if each of those passengers were to drive to work instead. These private motor cars changed the face of Britain's cities in many ways. Road signs, Belisha Beacons, white lines painted on the surface of the road, traffic lights; the list grew year by year.

Cars brought dramatic and not always welcome changes to the suburbs where the commuters lived as well. As the traffic built up in the so-called 'ribbon developments' along newly built-up country roads, then an obvious solution suggested itself. Why not simply construct a road just for the cars; one which would bypass the built-up areas? This would reduce the number of accidents, while simultaneously allowing traffic to flow more quickly. The new 30-mile-an-hour speed limit which had been introduced in 1934 applied only to built-up areas. The bypass would not be affected by this and drivers could fairly whiz around the edges of cities and towns without having to worry about such things as the new pedestrian crossings with their bright orange globes, which gave right of way to those crossing the road.

Those building bypasses in the 1930s were pursuing the same chimera as planners today who hope that ring roads and motorways will alleviate traffic congestion. The simple fact is that traffic will increase to fill up any available road and within a short space of time, there will be a need for a new bypass to bypass the old bypass, which has become one long traffic jam, and the process will begin anew. One need only look at the construction of the M25 motorway around London. Traffic jams and gridlocks became a feature of this road almost as soon as it was opened and work is now afoot to add extra lanes to it. Of course, no sooner are they completed, than they too will be filled to capacity. Car ownership was growing at a fantastic rate from the 1920s onwards and no road building schemes could hope to keep pace with the number of new vehicles on the roads. By 1950 there were 2.26 million private cars in Britain, by 1970 the number had risen to 11.51 million and by the end of the twentieth century, there were no fewer than 26.5 million cars on the country's roads. Nor has the number yet stabilised, let alone fallen. At the last count 32 million private vehicles were registered in Britain.

Commuters were a major driving force behind the relentless growth in car ownership which began in the years between the two world wars. The new ribbon developments were partly to blame. Anybody wishing to move into one of the smart, semi-detached houses in these formerly remote and isolated new communities would be well advised to buy a car, there being few public transport links. This was tacitly encouraged by those building such rows of houses, as they often incorporated garages. There was a good deal of status-seeking going here, with the commuting middle managers who could afford to move into such houses seeing themselves perhaps as the heirs of the Victorian man of property who could afford to run his own carriage. It was a matter of pride to such people that they did not need to rely upon buses or trains. We shall return to this idea shortly.

The ribbon developments which were springing up around cities and large towns had a way of proliferating as new bypasses were built. Inevitably, houses began to be erected along the bypasses themselves, turning them into built-up areas and so triggering the 30-mile-an-hour speed limit which was automatically imposed upon such districts, which in turn required a new bypass to be constructed to avoid these new urban areas. A natural consequence of this piecemeal and haphazard development taking place on the edges of large cities, was what came to be known as 'urban sprawl'. The cities spilled over into the countryside, throwing out tentacles of ribbon developments and bypasses like so many hungry octopuses, engulfing and strangling fields, farms and villages in the process. This was of course how some cities had come into being in the first place; places like Birmingham and Manchester. There was no appetite though, in the twentieth century, to see this happen again and to watch cities joining up into mega-conurbations, as their growing suburbs met. It was cars which were helping to drive this expansion. Rather than needing to wait until new railway or bus links were established, those building the new houses could see that in the future, such things might become an irrelevance.

Even before the outbreak of the Second World War, thought was being given to ways in which this headlong rush for urban growth might be checked. All the talk of ribbon developments suggested the name for the remedy, which was to be a so-called 'green ribbon', which would encircle cities and towns and restrict any further expansion. The expression 'green ribbon' did not really catch on and today, we know these areas of countryside where building is forbidden or restricted, as 'Green Belts'. These Green Belts were to have a profound effect upon commuting; initially, at least, acting to deter any rise in the numbers of commuters. This was because as the Green Belt policy was given a statutory foundation, the government which put it in place attempted to set up new developments which would render the very need for commuting redundant.

As early as 1935, the suggestion was being made that a limit should be placed on the growth of London by forbidding building or other development beyond the current limit of the suburbs. It was not until the passing of the Town and Country Planning Act 1947 though, that local authorities were given the power to designate areas around their towns and cities as Green Belts. The establishment of green belts was enthusiastically adopted, until today green belts account for no less than 13 per cent of the total area of England. One curious point is immediately noticeable when examining a map of Green Belts. We have seen in earlier chapters that the areas where accessible reefs of coal are to be found were where the Industrial Revolution was most vigorous. These same parts of the country were also where the highest rates of infant mortality were, in the nineteenth century, as well as also being the locations of the longest networks of municipal trams. Those regions are also where England's Green Belts have been set up; around London, Birmingham, Newcastle, Stoke-on-Trent and in an arc stretching from Liverpool, through Manchester and Leeds, down to Nottingham.

At about the same time that legislation made it possible for councils to put Green Belts around their urban areas, the government in the years following the end of the Second World War, tried in a sense to arrange communities where commuting would be quite unnecessary. This was to be achieved by the setting up of new towns. Massive conurbations were coming to be seen as undesirable for many reasons and it was thought that more manageable towns on a smaller scale might be in some way more 'human' than simply allowing people to be packed tighter and tighter in existing urban areas. With big cities like London and Manchester, which had been growing outwards at such an alarming rate for so many years; commuting was really an inevitable by-product of the growth. Obviously, not everybody could live near to their places of work.

The New Towns Act of 1946 allowed the government to designate an area as a new town and provide for its development. Some of the new towns were in a ring around London, others were scattered about other parts of the country. All were intended to be self-contained and planned communities, with schools, shopping centres and industry all carefully mapped out before a brick was laid. There was to be nothing random and haphazard about these towns. In existing cities, people had to travel miles to take their children to school or to get to work. In new towns such as Harlow and Milton Keynes, everything would be a short walk or cycle-ride from one's home.

The theory behind the new towns which were dotted about the country in the years following the end of the Second World War was faultless. There was little to be said for living ten or eleven miles from where you worked, so residential, commercial and industrial zones would be carefully planned so that long journeys to work would no longer be necessary. Ideally, people would live within a mile or two of their workplaces. This was certainly how it was meant to be with new towns in Essex, such as Harlow and Basildon. Harlow had only 4,000 residents in its early years and was a neat and compact community situated just outside London's Green Belt.

Today, towns such as Harlow and Basildon are regarded primarily not as self-contained communities, but rather as commuter towns, whose residents will travel to work in London. They have become in effect detached suburbs of London and their chief attraction is that property prices are somewhat lower than in London itself. Despite being planned as compact urban districts where one could walk to walk or the shops, ownership of cars in these 'New Towns' is now essential.

The use of cars for commuting is more than just a convenient means of transport. In the nineteenth century, travelling to work by bus was definitely a matter of status. The middle classes rode in buses, which were, by and large, too expensive for working men. Later on, the trams became a distinctly working-class means of commuting. Those hoping to appear to belong to the middle class avoided trams and instead took the bus, one reason for the demise of the tram and its replacement by trolleybuses. Today, the situation with buses is completely altered; travelling by bus entailing a definite loss of status. One is reminded of the statement which has been attributed, almost certainly erroneously, to Margaret Thatcher; 'A man who, beyond the age of 26, finds himself on a bus can count himself a failure.'

In Mr Pooter's day, one could travel to Town by bus in the morning and be reasonably sure that fellow passengers would be only commuters of roughly the same social level; i.e. professionals and officer workers. Such a journey might perhaps be similar these days to travelling first class on a train; status, combined with the assurance of not being compelled to mingle with lower class people. By the 1950s, all this had changed. The Tube was all one class and everybody used buses. That exclusively working-class means of public transport, the tram, was vanishing from British cities. All commuters were reduced to sharing the same methods of public transport; except of course, those with cars.

Here was the real status symbol among commuters of the post-war years. Impervious to railway strikes, unaffected by suicides on the Underground and, best of all, not being forced to rub shoulders with the 'wrong' sort of passenger. Those who drove to work in the first decade or two following the end of the Second World War could be very supercilious towards less-fortunate colleagues, the car conferring the social cachet which had once been enjoyed by the Victorian man of business who could afford to run his own horse and carriage. This exclusivity could not of course last, but while it did, it was intoxicating. The dramatic rise in car ownership during the 1950s made it inevitable that the number of those commuting to work in this way would increase steeply, but even so one still belonged to a club which enabled one to look down with lordly disdain upon fellow workers who were still wholly reliant upon the buses and Tube.

By the 1960s many in North America, along with a growing number in Britain, had come to feel almost naked without their cars. The idea for such people of catching a bus to work would have been unthinkable. Marshall McLuhan, the Canadian thinker who coined the expression 'global village', wrote in 1964: 'The car has become an article of dress without which we feel uncertain, unclad and incomplete in the urban compound.' This pretty well sums up the case to this day and goes some way towards explaining why driving is today far and away the most popular way of getting to work in this country.

Quite apart from the convenience (and the convenience of driving around and parking in British cities today must surely be open to question), there is the desire to avoid at all costs being seen as dependent on buses or other forms of public transport. Surely, only a failure would be caught dead queuing at a bus stop, the bus having taken over the role which the tram once had in Britain, of being a way of travelling restricted solely to the old, poor and unsuccessful.

What of the present situation with regard to commuting by car? Still looking at figures from the 2011 census, the proportion of people using private motor vehicles to get to work, either as drivers or passengers, is about 60 per cent in England and Wales. The figure is somewhat different though if we consider genuine commuters, those travelling some way to get to work. Looking first at London, we see at once that fewer than 30 per cent of people use cars to get to work. Those travelling by car to get to work in London are greatly outnumbered by people who travel by rail or bus. This is quite logical really, because of course the capital has the best transport links to be found anywhere in the country. If you work in the City of London and live practically next-door to a Tube station in the suburbs, it would be perverse to insist on jumping in the car and struggling along the congested streets to the office by that means instead. There is, unsurprisingly, a direct and strong correlation between the availability of public transport and its use to get to work. In London, where there are bus stops, Tube stations and suburban railway stations at every street corner, half of all workers use public transport to get to their place of work. In the South West of England, where rail services are pricy and bus routes patchy, just 6.3 per cent travel to work in this way.

There are signs that driving to work is on the decline, although the fall in numbers is not dramatic; except in London. In 2001, 55.2 per cent of people drove to work; the 2011 figure was 54.2 per cent. In London though, the drop was far more noticeable. In 2001, 33.5 per cent of workers were driving to work, but ten years later, this was down to 26.3 per cent; which looks like a distinct trend.

Chapter 12

Strap-hangers and the Rush Hour: The Etymology of Commuting

We saw in the Introduction that the word 'commuter' was a back formation from 'commutation'; as used in the expression 'commutation ticket'. The origin of that term, which was an Americanism, is of some interest. The word 'commute' itself, which was in use 500 years ago, means interchanging two things, from the Latin *commutare* formed by adding *com*, meaning together, to *mutare*, which means 'to change'. For at least two hundred years in America, 'commutation' has been used to mean reducing something, whether a prison sentence or the cost of a ticket. An early example of its use in the latter sense may be found in an advertisement from a little over two centuries ago.

In 1814, a poster appeared in New York, urging the residents of that city to use the steam ferry which was running between Brooklyn and Manhattan. As an inducement, 'commutation tickets' were offered for those who wished to pay in advance for eight months or a year. This advertisement was couched in the most obscure language imaginable, saying that: 'Such persons as are inclined to compound, agreeable in law, in the Steam Ferry-Boat, Barges, or common Horse Boats, will be pleased to apply to the subscribers, who are authorised to settle the same.' A ticket valid for eight months cost $6.67 and one for a year, $10.

Such commutation tickets were of course what we would today call season tickets and it was the coming of the railways to America which brought about the widespread use of commutation tickets in cities such as New York, Boston and Chicago. The back-formation of the words 'commuting' and 'commuter' followed. Surprisingly, it was to take a century for these very useful expressions to cross the Atlantic and become common in Britain.

Those who lived some distance from the heart of a city, but travelled to work every day by public transport were, just as in the USA, entitled to a reduction in the price of their fares, but in Britain, such individuals were known until the end of the Second World War not by the vulgar Americanism of 'commuter', but by the altogether more respectable appellation of 'season ticket holders'.

There is something about 'season ticket holders' which sounds far more solid and worthy than mere 'commuters' ever could. A season ticket holder is likely to be a man of substance, a businessman able to afford an annual ticket, paying his way in advance. He was apt to be of more consequence than somebody who just happened to travel to work by Tube or train. This at least was the psychological impediment to season ticket holders allowing themselves to be described as commuters.

The change in nomenclature was shockingly swift. In 1945, you would have been hard-pressed to find anybody in Britain willing to be thought of as a commuter: by 1960, it was season ticket holders who had become a vanished breed. The linguistic triumph was so rapid and complete, that in 1963 *The Times* was lamenting the passing of the season ticket holder, whom they described as, 'An ample, solid citizen, going about his business with a complacent knowledge of his status'. The fact was, there were so many people travelling into the cities and towns of Britain each day to work after the end of the war, that a shorter expression needed to be coined, 'season ticket holder' being too much of a mouthful for the younger generation. All else apart, with so many people now travelling to work by car, a catch-all expression was needed for all those who had to go some distance to get to work; including the many who did so without using public transport at all.

It was confusing at first to find the word 'commuter', which of course meant originally somebody with a season ticket to travel on public transport, being freely used to describe the drivers of private motor vehicles. Once 'commuter' had supplanted 'season ticket holder' to describe workers using trains and buses though, the word quickly became a general term applying to anybody travelling some distance to his or her workplace. In recent years, the term has become even more widely applied and is now used to refer to any sort of journey to work; however brief. The Office for National Statistics, for instance, talks easily of 'Commuting Patterns in the UK, 2011' and then make it clear that they are actually discussing simply getting to work. When mention is made of the fact that those working in car factories have, on average, only a 20-minute journey to get to their place of work, it is hard to see that as being commuting in the sense that most of us think of it. In the future, it is altogether possible that the word 'commuter' will be so diluted as to be essentially meaningless if this trend continues.

It is easy to fall into the error of supposing 'suburbs', like 'commuters' to be of relatively late usage in Britain, but the case is quite different. The first recorded use of the word in England was as early as 1380. References to the suburbs are found scattered throughout Shakespeare's plays, which suggests strongly that it was a word which those watching his plays would readily have understood. In Act 2, Scene 1 of *Julius Caesar*, we find Portia reproaching her husband Brutus by asking rhetorically, 'Dwell I but in the suburbs of your good pleasure? If it be no more, then Portia is Brutus' harlot, not his wife'. The audience must have been familiar enough with the ordinary meaning of the word, in order to appreciate its metaphorical use in this context. In *Twelfth Night* Shakespeare uses suburbs in the more literal sense, when he has Antonio advise Sebastian that, 'The best place to stay around here is an inn called the Elephant, in the suburbs south of the city'.

Our word 'suburb' is ultimately derived from the Old French 'subburbe', which in turn comes from the Latin *suburbium*, meaning under or below the city. In ancient Rome, the aristocracy lived on the hills, while those of less worth had to make do with the lower ground. It is curious to note that the singular form of the word 'suburbs', which is to say referring to a 'suburb', was at one time considered to be an illiteracy in English. This is because of its Latin derivation. Just as some pedants object to the formation of split infinitives, on the grounds that splitting the infinitive form of a verb is not possible in Latin, so too was the point raised when suburbs came to be a common word, that it was not a plural at all and therefore to back-form a singular form by dropping the letter 'S' from the end, showed a lamentable ignorance of the Latin language. The 'urbs' part of the word 'suburbs' is formed from the Latin word for city. It is not a plural form at all, but a word in its own right. Adding it as a suffix to 'sub' and then regarding the word thus formed as being a plural, was therefore barbarous and wrong.

In modern Britain, 'suburban' is of course something more than a neutral adjective. It can also be a pejorative term, used to dismiss a certain lifestyle, primarily that associated with commuters. Indeed, even the *Oxford English Dictionary* recognises this, by giving two very different definitions for the word as being either, on the one hand, 'of or characteristic of a suburb', and on the other, 'contemptibly dull and ordinary'. This secondary meaning, which has by association come to tar not only those living in the suburbs but also commuters, has only been in use since the late 1950s. The explicit use of the word 'suburban' to denote a dull lifestyle may only have been with us for a few decades, but the idea itself was common in Victorian times.

In *The Diary of a Nobody*, Mr Pooter and his wife are invited to dine at an acquaintance's house. Among the other guests that evening is Hardfur Huttle, 'a very clever writer for the American papers'. Mr Huttle unwittingly, and rather tactlessly, begins to talk about the way of life followed by the suburban dinner guests; most of whom are commuters. He denounces the suburban life in no uncertain terms, expressing the view that 'happy medium' is another way of saying 'miserable mediocrity'. In a sustained assault upon the *mores* of those with whom he is dining, Huttle says: 'The happy medium is nothing more or less than a vulgar half-measure. A man who loves champagne and, finding a pint too little, fears to face a whole bottle and has recourse to an imperial pint, will never build a Brooklyn Bridge or an Eiffel Tower. No, he is half-hearted, he is a half-measure – respectable – in fact, a happy medium, and will spend the rest of his days in a suburban villa with a stucco-column portico, resembling a four-post bedstead.' Hardfur Huttle's views and opinions on suburban life resonate with Mr and Mrs Pooter, reminding them powerfully of their son Lupin's attitude towards their quiet life in the suburb of Holloway. The idea of suburban life and the commuting lifestyle being somehow dull and boring has evidently been around for some while.

Another of those phrases which, although ostensibly bland, have a deeper meaning is 'nine to five', often used to describe office workers in particular. We know, from both diaries and other records of the time, that the usual hour for clerical workers to be at their office was, from at least as early as 1820; nine in the morning. The Eight-Hour Day Movement which arose after the Industrial Revolution was aimed at securing the same hours of work for manual workers and labourers as those who worked in offices enjoyed. Such men began at nine, worked for eight hours and then finished at five in the afternoon. Nine to five has therefore been a regular feature of life for British officer workers for two centuries or so. It is for this reason that we tend to see 'nine to five' as being synonymous with office jobs or other white-collar employment.

All commuters will be familiar with the expressions 'strap-hanger' and 'rush hour', meaning respectively a standing passenger on the Tube, bus or train, and the peak period of travel for commuters in the morning and evening. Like commuter, strap-hanger is an importation from the United States. Originally, it had the quite specific meaning of somebody standing during a journey by public transport, but it is now used in the wider sense of being applied to commuters generally who travel by train or bus. We note this extension and overuse of a specific term relating to commuting even with the very word 'commuter'. Although this was originally coined to describe those holding season tickets for public transport, by the 1960s, even drivers were being included in the general category of 'commuters'. So too with strap-hangers, which term gradually came to embrace not only standing passengers, but all those who regularly used public transport to get to work.

One of the earliest examples of the use of the term 'strap-hangers' includes also another phrase which will be familiar to any commuter; that of the 'rush hour'. Page 7 of the 22 February 1896 edition of the *Chicago Daily Tribune* carried a piece about the trials and tribulations of being a commuter in the city and included the following quotation: '"No sane man," said a Northsider yesterday who has been a strap-hanger for years, "expects the street car lines to furnish seats for every passenger during the rush hour morning and evening".' The casual use of both expressions suggests strongly that 'strap-hanger' and 'rush hour' were already at that time well-known enough to need no explanation. It is reasonable to assume therefore, that long before the beginning of the twentieth century, strap-hanging and rush hours were regarded as occupational hazards of the commuter; at least in America.

An earlier reference to the rush hour may be found than that above, in the *Street Railway Journal* for 1892, where a writer says that: 'The committee's study has been confined to the rush hour between 5:30 and 6:30 pm.' During the 1890s, the term was not applied only to public transport, but was used generally to describe an exceptionally busy period occurring at a particular time, for instance in restaurants and bars. It was only as the twentieth century drew on that the more specific meaning, that of relating to the crowds of commuters in the mornings and evenings, became the only one for which 'rush hour' was used. Some English strap-hangers during the rush hour may be seen in Illustration 20.

We have already examined in some detail the origins of the word 'bus', still a popular method of transport for commuters. Although this is the most logical abbreviation from the longer word, it took some little time to become established in that spelling and for many years, there were proponents of the alternative spelling of 'buss'. Dictionaries in Britain gave 'buss' as the correct version until the middle of the nineteenth century, when a gradual acceptance of 'bus' replaced it. The use of the double 'S' version lingers on though in the plural form and both 'buses' and 'busses' are still technically correct, although 'busses' is now almost entirely restricted to North America.

A curious point of pedantry associated with the word 'bus' is the prefixing of the word with an apostrophe, to indicate that some letters of the word have been omitted. This is found in *The Diary of a Nobody*, of course, but continued to be regarded as correct, if a little fussy, well into living memory. A 1971 edition of *Chambers Twentieth Century Dictionary* gives both 'bus' and ''bus' as being the correct spelling. Much the same thing happened of course with the word 'telephone', with the abbreviation ''phone' being written with an apostrophe in front being regarded as the more correct form until a few decades ago.

Other nations might have metros or subways, but the underground railway in London has been known, for well over a century, as the 'Tube'. The first use in Britain of the word 'tube' to describe a railway tunnel dates back to 1847, but it was not until 1864 that the word began to be used to refer to a railway system itself. This was the year that a pneumatic railway line was set up in the gardens surrounding the Crystal Palace in South London. This really was a tube line, although it only ran for a third of a mile, connecting the low-level and high-level railway stations near Crystal Palace. The carriages were propelled through a sealed tube by compressed air driven by a gigantic fan powered by a steam engine. Although the City and South London Railway, which opened in 1890, was sometimes referred to as a 'tube' railway, the widespread use of the word for the whole of London's rapidly-growing underground railway network began only when the *Daily Mail* coined the phrase, 'The Twopenny Tube' for the Central Line when it opened in 1900. From that year onwards, the 'Tube' was what Londoners called their underground railway, and still do to this day. The *Daily Mail* had something of a knack for coining new words and expressions at that time. It was that same newspaper which, on 10 January 1906, came up with the word used ever since to describe the more militant type of agitator for female suffrage. The word 'suffragette' has ever since been used for the members of that campaign.

Discussion of the word 'tube' might be a good place to dispose of one of the most enduring urban legends about the London Underground, which is that long ago a woman gave birth on an Underground train and decided to have her baby christened Thelma Ursula Beatrice Eleanor; this giving the acronymous initials; T.U.B.E. There is not a word of truth in the story, the baby being born on the Tube train in 1924 actually being called Marie Cordery. It makes for a nice story though!

Using the capitalised word 'Underground' as a proper noun began almost as soon as the Metropolitan Railway's services began. The first public underground trains in London ran on Saturday 10 January 1863. The novel *Vice Versa*, mentioned in Chapter 3, was published in June 1882, a shade under twenty years after the first Underground services began. Already though, the use of *the* Underground, as a noun, rather than an adjective, is seen. The protagonist fainted and came to in a Hansom cab. He is confused and wonders how he got home that day: 'Could it be another delusion, too, or was it the fact that he had found himself much pressed for time and had come home by the Underground to Praed Street?'

The use of the definite article is significant, because it shows that the transformation of the word from adjective to proper noun is an accepted figure of speech by this time. Until that time, 'underground' had been either an adverb or adjective; depending upon context. This position was formalised in 1908, when the word 'Underground' began appearing on posters and station signs in London.

Thinking still of that first underground railway in the world, reminds us that it actually gave its name to all other such systems which have since been established across the globe the Metropolitan Railway was the prototype and progenitor of them all. In the late nineteenth century, when the French were toying with the idea of burrowing under the streets of Paris and excavating an underground railway there of their own, a company was set up to go about the business. This was called *La Compagnie du chemin de fer métropolitain de Paris,* which translates as 'The Paris Metropolitan Railway Company'. When it opened in 1900, the name was soon abbreviated to the Metropolitan for short and then truncated even further, until people referred simply to the 'Metro'. In time, the word 'Metro' came to be used for all underground railway systems across the world; from Moscow to Mexico City. All are therefore named ultimately after that first underground railway, London's own Metropolitan Line.

Chapter 13

Gentrification, Densification and the End of the Commuter

It is time to consider the present state of, and future prospects for, commuting in Britain. Several trends emerge from such an analysis, all of which point, rather disconcertingly, in different directions. So contradictory are the signals for future trends in commuting that to make sense of things we shall need to examine some aspects of the matter in detail.

First, it is undeniably true that there are, by any definition, more commuters in the country now than has ever before been the case. Not only that, but there is a rising tendency to go in for what some define as 'extreme commuting': which is to say commuting which entails a journey of more than an hour and a half to get to work. From this perspective, commuting is thriving as never before and over a third of people working in this country now commute, in the sense of living in one local authority area and working in another. The actual proportion of commuters in society has not risen noticeably in recent years, it is rather that the population of Britain has risen.

Set against the current popularity for the practice, there are signs that the peak in commuting has perhaps been reached and that the numbers of commuters could be on the cusp of declining. According to this reading of the situation, the sociological and demographic factors which brought about commuting in the first place, have largely vanished, and are indeed now operating in reverse. Before we examine these two opposing ideas, it might be time to introduce a third, even stranger notion for consideration; that the very existence of the commuter as an identifiable figure is in danger of disappearing entirely from Britain. This is chiefly a problem of semantics. Before examining this particular hypothesis, let us first deal with the indisputable fact that the actual practice of commuting is thriving in this country as never before.

The 2011 census provides a wealth of data on the working habits of men and women in Britain; including the ways in which they travel to and from their workplaces. Out of a total working population of around 30 million, 11,260,336 are commuters, according to the definition of living in one local authority area and working in another. As has been remarked before, a journey of some considerable distance must surely be the bare minimum for travel to work to be considered a bona fide commute. The essential point of commuting is that it involves a separation between the worlds of home and work. This separation is both geographical and psychological; the commuting journey being a period of adjustment between the two different spheres. For those living in a suburb and working in the centre of a city, this process is clear-cut and plain. The residential streets of the suburb or dormitory town contrast sharply with the bustle and hurly-burly of the commercial heart of a great city. The same can hardly be said of the man or woman who lives two or three streets from the factory or shop in which he or she works. The short drive or walk to work is all within the usual environment in which they live and it would be absurd to call this commuting to work.

Having seen that at least a third of the population are commuters, what grounds might we have for saying that the practice might be upon the verge of declining? One of the most significant developments in commuting in this country over the last fifty years or so has been the process known as 'gentrification'. This has seen shabby and rundown inner city areas becoming colonised by well-to-do middle class professionals who typically move there from the suburbs. Since this is precisely the opposite of the trend which first established commuting as a popular lifestyle in this country, it is interesting to see what motivation lies behind this drift back towards the centre of cities.

During the nineteenth century, the middle classes moved to smart suburbs and then abandoned them and moved further outwards as the areas where they lived became less desirable; which is to say, more working class. The consequence was that the further away from the city centre one moved, the smarter and more expensive became the district. The most posh suburbs always tended to be those on the outer extremity of cities; next to the open country.

The expression 'gentrification' is not a modern one. It has, rather surprisingly, been in circulation for over fifty years. The word was coined in 1964 by a British sociologist called Ruth Glass. She wrote about the displacement of working class residents from the London district of Islington, as middle-class professionals moved in and began renovating and restoring properties. As such areas became more 'up-market', so rents rose and property prices soared, which had the effect of driving poorer people out. The process accelerated until a formerly dilapidated and undesirable part of an inner city was transformed into the fashionable location to live. This is still happening today in British cities and is even more prevalent now than when Glass wrote about it in the 1960s.

Those who move to inner-city areas in this way usually have white-collar jobs in central areas and so, in effect, they cease to be commuters. Often, they are able to reach their offices by walking or perhaps cycling a short distance. No more reliance upon Tubes, buses and trains for them! It is the less well-off inhabitants who have been pushed out who are likely now to move further out of the city. The driving forces behind the return of middle-class commuters to the inner cities are complex. One or two of them tie in with ideas at which we have looked in previous chapters. We examined the way in which suburban life began to be viewed after the end of the Second World War as monotonous and dull; something to flee from, rather than embrace. This is one of the factors which led middle and upper-middle class people to wish to leave the suburbs and live right in the middle of a city. In the late 1960s and 1970s, the rejection of suburban life by artistic, intellectual and fashionable middle–class men and women led to the idea of 'inner city chic', that living in the heart of a city was somehow more authentic than being on the outer fringes. Some districts have undergone transformations of this sort several times over the last couple of centuries. We looked in an earlier chapter at Notting Hill and Holland Park, part of which was known in the mid-nineteenth century as the 'Potteries and Piggeries'. This was a district of slums. We saw how smart houses were built around there and the pig keepers and brick makers forced to move elsewhere. Later on, Notting Hill became one of the less fashionable suburbs, until it became once more a slum district; all the grand houses having been divided up into multiple occupancies. In the 1960s and 1970s, it underwent gentrification, until it is now one of the most expensive places to live in the whole of Britain.

This then is one reason that commuters move back towards the inner cities, because they despise suburban life and find living actually *in* a city and not on the edge of it, half in the countryside and half in a built-up area, far more satisfying. There are, after all, far more restaurants, theatres, cinemas, art galleries, good shops and cultural attractions to be found near the centre of a city than in even the best suburb. With luck, moving into the right gentrified district might mean that you are within easy walking distance of all these attractions.

Of course, living in the inner city as an 'urban pioneer' would not be nearly so attractive to an up and coming professional if it meant living in conditions such as those described by Engels when he was writing about the centre of Manchester in *The Condition of the Working Class in England*. Nobody wishes to live in an industrial wasteland. In recent years, we have seen the deindustrialisation of British cities. The power stations have closed down, the sweatshops have moved elsewhere, the gasworks are gone, as are most of the steel mills and factories. In short, the things which drove the middle classes away from the cities and forced them to become commuters in the first place have gone now. The poverty and crime which precipitated the so-called 'white flight' from inner cities during the 1970s has also declined. It is safe for respectable people to live once more in the inner cities! This has of course implications for the practice of commuting, for if people are both living and working in the same geographical area, the need for commuting will be liable to fade away. The first indications that this might be a coming development are to be found in London; but they are by no means restricted to the capital.

This move from the suburbs to the centres of cities is not limited to the gentrification of London districts such as Islington, Shoreditch and Brixton. It is part of a wider phenomenon which may be observed especially in the great cities which owe their very origins to the Industrial Revolution which gave birth to commuting in the first place. During the early years of the Industrial Revolution, the centres of cities such as Manchester, Liverpool and Birmingham became crammed to bursting point. The dreadful conditions which arose from this rapid and uncontrolled rise in population, triggered a flight to the edges of cities and the creation of suburbs. Once effective public transport was available, these suburbs grew rapidly and any study of differing population trends in various parts of individual cities in nineteenth-century Britain, would have shown that the suburbs were becoming more densely populated, while the number of people living in the centres of cities was slowly declining.

A quick glance at modern demographic maps of former industrial cities across the whole of Britain, shows that the prevailing tendency is now towards stable or declining populations in the suburbs and increasing 'densification', to use the technical term, in the centres. This can be seen in places as far apart as Sheffield, Glasgow, Birmingham, Cardiff, Liverpool and Leicester. Everywhere one looks, the increase in population density is in city centres and the decrease in the suburbs. Britain appears to be falling out of love with suburban life in a big way. One or two concrete examples might make this clearer. The Birmingham suburbs of West Bromwich and Sparkbrook show rapid decline in population, whereas the central district shows a marked rise. In Leeds, the trend is even more noticeable, with the outlying districts of Hyde Park and Bramley both showing declines, coupled again a sharp rise in population density in the centre. This movement towards higher populations in central districts is associated with, although not precisely similar to, the gentrification at which we have looked; the desire to live as close as possible to the centre of cities being very much a middle-class thing. The current situation in London shows clearly that this movement of population is based upon class and little else.

It has been described as 'social cleansing': the apparent flight of working class and ethnic minority families from inner London. It is the opposite of the 'white flight' which was seen in the 1970s and 1980s, as middle class families wished to be as far out in the suburbs as they could manage. Now, they are returning in force to the inner city. Defining anybody's class in Britain is a tricky business. How do we know that those moving from the suburbs to the inner cities are in fact middle class and not working class? One way is to look at eligibility for such benefits as free school meals, which goes hand-in-hand with deprivation and lower socio-economic status. Traditionally, parts of London like Southwark and Newham have been working-class environments where very few professional people would choose to live. We saw in an earlier chapter that West Ham, in the heart of Newham, was originally founded as a specifically working class suburb. In the last five years though, this has all been changing dramatically. Between 2010 and 2015, the number of pupils eligible for free school meals fell by 25 per cent in Southwark and 31 per cent in Newham. Since the overall population of these local authority areas is rising, the conclusion is inescapable: poorer people are moving out of the area. It seems likely too that they are moving into the suburbs. Just as the numbers of children entitled to free school meals is declining in places like Southwark, Camden and Newham, so it is rising in outer areas like Croydon and Merton. Whatever the reasons for this changing demographic, the implications for the future of commuting in Britain are significant.

The story of British commuting has really been the story of higher social classes trying to get away from those who are less well-off. However much we try to express this in fancy sociological jargon, this is what has always motivated commuters. Sometimes, this migration is from slums to suburbs, at other times from suburbs to the countryside and now, seemingly, from the suburbs back to the inner city. At each stage of the process, there is a trade-off between convenience for work and not living next door to the 'wrong' sort of neighbour. It is noticed, and incidentally greatly resented, by those living in inner-city areas which become gentrified, that the newcomers tend to stick together and avoid the local people who are already living there. They open their own shops, which are often too pricy for working-class people who might be on benefits, such organic health food outlets and so on, and establish their own culture, just as though they are colonising a backward country. This can lead to violent protests from those who feel that their home district is almost being colonised by wealthy, middle-class commuters. In September 2015, this kind of thing led to rioting on the streets of the London when a trendy café in London's Brick Lane was targeted by several hundred protestors who were angry about the gentrification of that part of the East End. The Cereal

Killer Café offered bowls of cornflakes for £3 to the middle-class types who were moving into Tower Hamlets. It was felt by some locals that shops and restaurants of this sort were driving out the smaller and cheaper places which ordinary working-class people wanted in their neighbourhood.

After a while, a tipping point is reached. As the area undergoing this gentrification becomes fashionable, property prices and rents rise and those who have been living there all their lives find themselves priced out of their own neighbourhood. They typically drift off to the suburbs. Clerkenwell, London's EC1 postcode area, was for centuries a rundown area where the very poorest lived. Dickens uses Clerkenwell in his novels to indicate the lowest and most deprived parts of the city. Fagin's den was in Clerkenwell and Dickens gives a vivid description of the streets in that part of London that the Artful Dodger leads Oliver to: 'A dirty and more wretched place he had never seen. The street was very narrow and muddy, and the air was impregnated with filthy odours.' In *Bleak House,* Phil Squod describes the tinker's beat which he had in that district, travelling the streets and offering to mend pots and pans: 'It wasn't much of a beat – round Saffron Hill, Hatton Garden, Clerkenwell and Smiffield and there – poor neighbourhood, where they uses up the kettles till they're past mending.' In short, Clerkenwell was just the sort of location that caused the beginning of commuting in the first place! People moved to the outer edges of London to escape the poverty and squalor of Clerkenwell and other inner city areas, putting up with the inconvenience of a long journeys as a small price to pay for being free of living near the place. At the time of writing, a two-bedroom flat is on offer in a converted school building in Clerkenwell. It is nothing grand, but the asking price is £1 million. In the same street, Chequer Street, not far from the Barbican, is another two-bedroom apartment, this one on offer for £2,695,000. The point of this is not simply the fabulous amounts of money necessary now to live in what was once an impoverished part of the capital, but that these flats are only half a mile from Liverpool Street Station and the Bank of England. Anybody living in a property of this sort and working in the City of London would no longer be a commuter at all, but would instead be living within a ten-minute walk of their place of work.

Some of the very wealthy are now abandoning the suburbs and returning to the centre of the cities. Nor is this trend limited to the enormously rich. Inner-city neighbourhoods such as Brixton in South London and Shoreditch, just north of the City of London, have in the last two decades or so seen an influx of young professionals who are not rich, but simply wish to live closer to the centre of London. The same thing is happening in other cities; Manchester, for example. Take the 47-storey Beetham Tower, which was completed in

2006. Located right in the heart of the city, the tower contains both an hotel and also 219 luxury apartments. Those with between £250,000 and £750,000 to spare flocked to live in a tower block right in the middle of Manchester. So keen were people to move into Beetham Tower that bidding wars broke out to secure the best of the flats. Here were men and women with plenty of money who had rejected for good and all the idea of the suburbs. Most would need only a five-minute walk to get to their offices from their new homes.

To recap, since the Industrial Revolution, the population shift in cities has been away from the centre and towards the outskirts; for reasons at which we have looked. This process continued unabated for two centuries or so. It was still a powerful factor in the years leading up to the Second World War; the suburban population of London increased by 1.5 million during the 1930s. During that same period, the population of inner London fell by half a million. Now, this historic tendency has been thrown into reverse. It is beyond the scope of a short book like this to explore all the reasons for this change in much detail. It is perhaps sufficient to say that the cities created during the Industrial Revolution are now often referred to as being 'post-industrial'. In other words, the industry has left the cities, leaving them cleaner and more attractive than they have ever been before. In London, porpoises and seals regularly swim up the Thames and are seen around the old Docklands. Other cities are in a similar state. With the factories, steel mills, docks and other industry having shrivelled away, there is no longer any reason for respectable and well-off people to shun the inner city.

Hand-in-hand with this trend for those who would naturally at one time have been suburban commuters to move inwards, rather than outwards, comes another and, on the face of it, puzzling trend; the increase in 'extreme commuting'. Of course, it will come as no surprise to discover that in rural areas adjoining London, many of the residents travel into the capital to work. In the Essex local authority area of Epping Forest, for instance, about 40 per cent of the inhabitants work in London. The fact that the London Underground runs straight into the heart of the Epping Forest area makes this fairly easy to understand. What about Cornwall and the isles of Scilly though, or the island of Anglesey, off the coast of North Wales? According to the 2011 census, 285 people commute regularly into Westminster or the City of London from Cornwall and the Scilly Isles. Another eighteen travel to work in those boroughs from Anglesey. These may perhaps be exceptional cases, but the overall numbers of extreme commuters is rising steeply. Taking the definition of an extreme commuter as one who travels for more than 90 minutes on the way to work and then home again in the evening, it is surprising to learn that 1.84 million workers are in this unenviable position, a substantial proportion of British commuters. The number has risen by 50 per cent in the space of five years.

Trying to work out the future of commuting in Britain is, because of the two diverging trends at which we have been looking, a tricky business. It is complicated even more by the fact that employment prospects have also changed in recent years. At one time, there were plenty of factories and office blocks in suburbs. Now, these are vanishing and being replaced by housing. This does not however appear to produce more commuters. In Ilford, a suburb at which we looked in some detail earlier, almost all the residents were, to begin with, young professionals, civil servants and commercial clerks and the whole area was based upon the commuting lifestyle. Now, only about a quarter of the borough's residents commute to central London.

It is time to look at a point raised earlier in this chapter, that the very existence of the commuter as an identifiable figure is now in doubt. This is because despite all the travelling to and from work which still takes place in this country, the very word 'commuter' is fast becoming so debased as to be practically meaningless. Indeed, one might justifiably claim that there really are no such people any more in Britain as commuters. On the other hand, one could assert, on similar grounds, that *everybody* is now a commuter. To understand this strange and counterintuitive notion, we must remember what we have so far learned about commuting and commuters.

We have seen how commuting began in a small way during the Industrial Revolution, with small numbers of people moving away from the centres of large cities and choosing to live on the of the city or in the neighbouring countryside. This custom grew over the nineteenth century and a recognisable type emerged; personified by fictional characters such as Mr Pooter or Jerome K. Jerome's Uncle Podger. Although not real people, they depicted faithfully a certain way of life. The commuter thus became a definite type of person, with whom everybody was familiar; even if they were not actually described as commuters until after the end of the Second World War. It was universally understood that these were men who lived in the suburbs or countryside and travelled into the commercial centres of cities; almost invariably by public transport. The commuter's natural habitat was the platform of railway stations. Use the word 'commuter' and it was to such a person one was understood to be referring.

No sooner had we begun to call these people who travelled a fair distance each day by public transport to get to work, 'commuters', rather than season ticket holders, than the word 'commuter' began to be more generally applied; for example to those who drove cars to work as well as those who used railways and buses. Commuters became men and women who travelled to work by any means. At the same time that this was happening, the archetypal commuter's appearance was changing. The bowler hat became rarer, the pinstripe suits and furled umbrellas faded away, until the stock image of the commuter, a man like the *Evening Standard*'s Bristow, was only to be found in cartoons and satirical television programmes.

From being a fairly exclusive and recognisable type, the commuter became indistinguishable from anybody else, until one could scan the crowds of passengers waiting at a suburban railway station without being able to hazard the least guess as to which were commuters heading for Town and which people merely going to the next station. The very idea of commuters in Britain is now essentially redundant; the word conveying no other meaning than somebody who works outside his or her home. The Office for National Statistics claims that over 80 per cent of the working population of the country are now regular commuters, basing this statement upon the fact that this is the proportion of men and women who work outside their own homes. Dictionaries too tell us that a commuter is somebody who travels 'some distance' to work. The word has thus become simply a synonym for somebody with a job outside the home. Commuting has come to mean just the journey to work, whether catching a train into Town from the suburbs or simply walking to a factory in the next street. We are all commuters now.

Over the last 200 years, the practice of commuting in this country has sprung up, spread and become an established way of life. For many years, the commuter was a readily recognisable type, so much so that he became a caricature. All this has now passed away. Standing at the foot of an escalator in a London tube station at half past five in the evening during the 1950s; one would have had no difficulty at all in distinguishing the commuters from other passengers such as tourists or shoppers. They were the ones wearing suits or smart skirts, carrying in their hands a copies of the *Evening News* or *Evening Standard*, the clean-shaven men carrying umbrellas and briefcases. Until relatively recently, commuting office-workers had always been more or less instantly recognisable in this way. We saw that Dickens had no difficulty identifying the 'clerk population' of Somerstown and Camden, as they made their way on foot to the city.

Any attempt today to pick out the commuters from the crowds rushing along in Holborn or near Liverpool Street Station would be a complete flop. True, some would be wearing suits, but the majority would not. These days, entrepreneurs of start-up companies which are doing very nicely are more likely to be wearing jeans and t-shirts and to have ponytails or designer stubble. Even the ordinary office worker no longer follows any readily-identifiable dress code. It is often impossible to distinguish the commuter from the tourist, to work out who works in an office and who has come up to Town for the evening to visit a cinema or take in a show.

The decline of the distinctive commuter, the person whose appearance tells one at once that he or she is a member of this group, combined with the modern redefining of what constitutes a commuter, suggests that it will not be long before the word 'commuter' ceases to have any sort of definite meaning at all, beyond that of a person who does not work at home. This would be a pity, because it would bring to an end a type who has been active in British cities for two centuries, people who have made a great and enduring contribution to the cultural and intellectual life of the country. When the day arrives that we are all commuters, then the commuter as a separate entity has in fact ceased to exist. Combined with the trends that have been examined in this chapter, it is altogether possible that this will be the last generation of commuters and that both the lifestyle and the word used to denote it will in another few years be no more than an historical curiosity.

Bibliography

Betjeman, John, *Collected Poems*, John Murray, 1958.

Bownes, David, Green, Oliver and Mullins, Sam, *Underground; How the Tube Shaped London*, Penguin Books, 2012.

Challoner, Jack (ed.), *1001 Inventions That Changed the World*, Cassell Illustrated, 2009.

Clayton, Antony, *Subterranean City: Beneath the Streets of London*, Historical Publishing, 2000.

Clout, Hugh (ed.), *The Times London History Atlas*, Times Books, 1991.

Cook, Chris and Stevenson, John, *The Longman Handbook of Modern British History 1714-1980*, Longman Group, 1983.

Curtis, Sue, *Ilford: A History*, Phillimore, 2004.

Evans, Brian, *Bygone Ilford*, Phillimore, 1989.

Farndon, John, *Dictionary of the Earth*, Dorling Kindersley, 1994.

Gardiner, Juliet, *The Thirties; An Intimate History*, HarperPress, 2010.

Glinert, Ed, *The London Compendium*, Alan Lane, 2003.

Harris, Melvin, *The Book of Firsts*, Michael O'Mara, 1994.

Hattersley, Roy, *Borrowed Time; The Story of Britain Between the Wars*, Little, Brown, 2007.

Hewson, Don, *Chadwell Heath and the Road to Romford Market*, Alan Sutton Publishing, 1995.

Jones, Edward and Woodward, Christopher, *A Guide to the Architecture of London*, George Weidenfeld & Nicolson, 1983.

Kynaston, David, *Austerity Britain 1945-51*, Bloomsbury Publishing, 2007.

Kynaston, David, *Modernity Britain 1957-62*, Bloomsbury Publishing, 2015.

Mitchell, R. J. and Leys, M. D. R., *A History of London Life*, Longmans, 1958.

Morgan, Kenneth (ed.), *The Oxford History of Britain*, Oxford University Press, 1984.

Palmer, Allan, *The East End*, John Murray, 1989.

Palmer, Douglas, *The Atlas of the Prehistoric World*, Marshall Publishing, 1999.

Priestley, J. B., *The Edwardians*, Heinemann, 1970.

Priestley, J. B., *English Humour*, Heinemann, 1976.

Robertson, Patrick, *The Shell Book of Firsts*, Ebury Press, 1974.

Sheppard, Francis, *London; A History*, Oxford University Press, 1998.

Slee, Christopher, *The Guinness Book of Lasts*, Guinness Publishing, 1994.

Sullivan, Frank and Winkowski, Fred, *Trams*, Quantum Publishing, 2003.

Sweet, Matthew, *Inventing the Victorians*, Faber and Faber, 2001.

Thorns, David (1972) *Surburbia* London, Paladin, 1972.

Trench, Richard and Hillman, Ellis, *London Under London*, John Murray, 1985.

Webb, Simon, *A 1960s East End Childhood*, The History Press, 2012.

Webb, Simon, *Not a Guide to Kensington and Chelsea*, The History Press, 2012.

Withington, John, *Capital Disasters*, Sutton Publishing, 2003.

Index